SHOES, GLUES, AND HOMEWORK

Dangerous Work in the Global Footwear Industry

Pia Markkanen

University of Massachusetts Lowell

Work, Health, and Environment Series
***Series Editors*: Charles Levenstein, Robert Forrant,
and John Wooding**

Routledge
Taylor & Francis Group

LONDON AND NEW YORK

First published 2009 by Baywood Publishing Company, Inc.

2 Park Square, Milton Park, Abingdon, Oxon OX14 4RN
711 Third Avenue, New York, NY 10017, USA

Routledge is an imprint of the Taylor & Francis Group, an informa business

First issued in paperback 2017

Library of Congress Catalog Number: 2009020469
ISBN 13: 978-0-89503-328-4 (hbk)

Library of Congress Cataloging-in-Publication Data

Markkanen, Pia, 1966-
   Shoes, glues, and homework : dangerous work in the global footwear industry / Pia Markkanen.
        p. ; cm. -- (Work, health, and environment series)
   Includes bibliographical references and index.
   ISBN 978-0-89503-328-4 (cloth : alk. paper)
   1. Footwear industry--Employees--Health and hygiene--Indonesia. 2. Footwear industry--Employees--Health and hygiene--Philippines. 3. Glue--Toxicology--Indonesia. 4. Glue--Toxicology--Philippines. 5. Home labor--Indonesia. 6. Home labor--Philippines. 7. Work environment--Indonesia. 8. Work environment--Philippines. I. Title. II. Series : Work, health, and environment series.
   [DNLM : 1. Adhesives--adverse effects--Indonesia. 2. Adhesives--adverse effects--Philippines. 3. Occupational Health--Indonesia. 4. Occupational Health--Philippines. 5. Health Policy--Indonesia. 6. Health Policy--Philippines. 7. Industry--standards--Indonesia. 8. Industry--standards--Philippines. 9. Shoes--economics--Indonesia. 10. Shoes--economics--Phillippines. WA 465 M345s 2009]
   HD9787 .I552.M37 2009
   363. 19--dc22

                                                                    2009020469

ISBN 978-0-89503-328-4 (hbk)
ISBN 978-0-415-78437-5 (pbk)

Table of Contents

Preface   v
   Charles Levenstein, Robert Forrant, and John Wooding

Introduction   xiii

CHAPTER 1
   The Structure of the Global Footwear Industry   1

CHAPTER 2
   Shoemaking and its Hazards   23

CHAPTER 3
   Informal Sector, Informal Economy   45

CHAPTER 4
   Does Gender Matter?   65

CHAPTER 5
   Shoe Chemicals and Right-to-Know   83

CHAPTER 6
   The Way Forward   89

Index   99

In Praise   103

Preface

This series of studies was launched at the beginning of a new millennium and, even then, it was clear that the brave talk of a new era was destined to remain nothing more than the empty rhetoric of promises unfulfilled. Around the world, workers and communities are increasingly the victims of dangerous workplaces and polluted environments. In all countries, too many people remain without jobs or under-employed. And with the global financial system in disarray, the tension between jobs and health is even more exacerbated.

In the United States many workers need more than one job to lift themselves beyond the poverty level, as the jobless numbers escalate. In much of Europe, unemployment rates appeared to be intractably high and, we fear, are likely to become even worse. In Asia and much of the developing world, workers slave in workplaces at wages that are appalling low and under conditions that threaten their lives and those of their families. In Africa, ravaged by AIDS and war, only the lucky few can put bread on the table.

Across the globe the threat of environmental catastrophe, the erosion of indigenous cultures, and the exploitation of workers continues unabated. Recurrent economic, social, and environmental crises threaten those among us who have made small gains. Illusionary stability can only be achieved with loans from the International Monetary Fund and the World Bank that come with stringent conditions to curtail even the minimal workplace and environmental health and safety regulations that may be in place. In the era of the so-called "triumph of the market" all is not well.

Pia Markkanen's extraordinary, first-hand investigation of the dangers of home work in the shoe industry in the Philippines and Indonesia is an important contribution to our understanding of work, health, and the global economy. She also carefully documents the intersection of gender relations and hierarchy with the social relations of "globalized" economic development and reveals the important implications for the health of women, men, and children as toxic work enters the home.

v

The book is particularly important because gender is too frequently not discussed by occupational health and safety investigators. The disruption of the traditional household by an invasive market capitalism has important implications for the psychological and social health of women and the family. Traditional or modern methods of political participation—trade unions, political parties—may not be open to women in developing countries and they therefore may be without a formal voice in political discussion about development. New forms of participation are developing for women— political, social, even entrepreneurial—which have important implications for health and development. For analytical and ethical reasons, Markkanen has seen that gender requires careful attention. Home work in the shoe industries of the Philippines and Indonesia provides her with an excellent lens through which to examine issues related to gender and work in the global economy.

To be sure medical advances and public health initiatives have reduced the fear of disease and early death for many. Standards of living have improved for some, and the awareness of threats to health and environment has made many more workers willing to fight for healthy lives. But much remains to be done, especially when the "free marketeers" minimize the role that democracy and government play in protecting the lives of citizens throughout the world. The "market" will never solve all of these problems.

So, does this mean that there is nothing we can do? Of course not. Rather, it means that we have an especially difficult task ahead. We must understand this era with good analysis and innovative strategies. We cannot look back to a golden progressive age or halcyon socialist past, nor can we forget the lessons we learned. What we must do is engage and understand what is going on in the world, and develop and propose viable alternatives and pro- gressive strategies. This in essence is the purpose of this book series and the point of our focus. Pia Markkanen's work ensures that gender and family are not neglected in this approach.

This book series begins at the point of production. Work is essential to all our lives. Work is where things are made, good things as well as bad things. While work brings income and meaning, it also brings danger and threats to health. The point of production is where goods and services are produced but it is also the source of environmental contamination and pollution. In other words, work, health, and environment are intimately linked. In this series authors analyze and describe the relationship between what goes on in the workplace, the consequences for the public health, and environ- mental degradation. We define health and environment broadly. Health is not limited to the absence of disease or to individual health. It must also mean a healthy and sustainable economy, a democratic and participatory politics, a workplace where the rights of workers are respected and enforced, and communities that are sustainable, crime free and nurturing of the physical and mental health of all. Finally, to achieve such sustainability, it is essential that we give appropriate attention to gender and family in social and economic development.

Charles Levenstein, Robert Forrant,
and John Wooding

Figure 1. Preparing footwear patterns in Thailand, in 2001. Photo by the author.

Figure 2. Preparing footwear patterns in Thailand, in 2001. Photo by the author.

Figure 3. Gluing and priming footwear soles in Thailand, in 2001. Photo by the author.

Figure 4. Gluing and priming footwear soles in Thailand, in 2001. Photo by the author.

Introduction

My first visit to a home-based shoe workshop in Thailand, in 2001, was an epiphany. The visit was the first chance I had to observe how the global market turns homes into manufacturing sites. It appeared that I had arrived in a residential neighborhood with apartment units in three and four story buildings. But a shoe workshop was tucked away in one of the units. At the front door, stacks of shoeboxes were ready to be transported to a subcontractor.

At the street level floor were two women sitting cross-legged on the floor cleaning and polishing dozens of pairs of shoes. On the second floor workers toiled surrounded by raw materials, boxes, tools, cooking equipment, glue cans, sewing machines, finished and unfinished shoes, and electrical wiring. Some of them ate a meal, drank a cup of coffee, or smoked cigarettes amid the clutter. As pieceworkers, they could not step away to eat. Some mothers had children with them. The clutter represented a serious fire hazard, and toxic fumes emanated from open glue bowls, glue containers, and cleaning and polishing chemicals. Little by little, reality unfolded. Home-based footwear manufacturing is fraught with serious safety, health, and environmental hazards. Perhaps, because I am a chemical engineer, chemical safety practices captivate me. The International Labour Organization's (ILO) project on the Elimination of Child Labour (IPEC) in the footwear sector wanted me to explore why the adhesives used in shoe manufacturing are hazardous solvent-based ones as opposed to available safer water-based ones. Reading the labels on the adhesive containers I found that most of them nicely explained how to apply the product to get a solid bond; none of them provided information how to use the solvent safely and about the ingredients, and their health effects. Workers had never heard about material safety data sheets (MSDSs). Soon, I witnessed comparable conditions in Indonesia and the Philippines. After observing over 50 shoe workshops I concluded that working conditions in the informal shoe production economy are extraordinarily dangerous (see Figures 1, 2, 3, and 4, pp. viii-xi).

The places where people in developing countries live have become home factories where a variety of goods are produced in very hazardous conditions. Shoes are an example of such home-produced goods. All family members— wives, husbands, and children—may participate in the shoe production and be exposed to solvents, dusts, and a range of other hazards. Because home-based shoemaking belongs to the informal economy, its workforce remains largely beyond the reach of the labor protection laws, social security benefits, and systematic labor union organizing efforts. Nevertheless, when home becomes the work environment, public and workplace health concerns converge. Even though safety and health in the informal economy have been increasingly addressed by various international organizations and academic research projects during the past decade, life-threatening hazards still do not get the attention they deserve considering that the informal sector employs the majority of the world's labor force.

The purpose of this book is to describe working conditions in informal sector shoemaking in Indonesia and the Philippines, their gender dimensions, and national and international policy implications. Qualitative investigation techniques were applied during October–December 2002, including 52 in-depth interviews, more than 50 shoe workshop walk-through inspections by local evaluators and the author. The findings of this study sketch an overall picture how various forces—local and international—influence work environment in informal sector shoemaking.

The use of organic solvents—in particular adhesives, primers, and cleaning agents—makes the shoe manufacturing sector a particularly hazardous occupation. This study illustrates an example of the global need for safer and healthier chemical alternatives and the necessity to introduce them at the beginning of all use and supply chain applications. At the same time, the study presents the complexity of the problem when considering safer alternatives substitution at the source. Hazardous chemicals cannot be controlled efficiently by those at the bottom of the production.

Use of chemicals in home-based production is not limited to shoe-making— it is just one example how global markets have introduced chemicals, materials, and production processes into developing nations. In societies where the majority of the population earns a living through the informal sector, and where the industrial and governmental infrastructures are weak, chemicals are often used in settings where socio-economic disparities—in particular poverty—facilitate the acceptance of dangerous practices. These health, safety, and environmental consequences can be tragic and will have serious global impacts.

The informal shoe production industry provides a snapshot of the risks and driving forces associated with the use of toxic chemicals. Globalized markets have produced situations where major chemical use and disposal occurs in some countries while final product consumption occurs in others. The challenge for eliminating or minimizing chemical hazards is to link local and regional conditions to effective preventive programs at an international level of chemicals management.

CHAPTER 1

The Structure of the Global Footwear Industry

Shoemaking is one of the most globalized industries. It is a model of interdependencies among people, communities, and nations linked through the global networks (McMichael, 2004). Footwear manufacturing may occur in a variety of production settings: mechanized factories, craft work or sub-contracting practices in small workshops which are often home-based. The vast majority of the world's footwear has been made in developing countries in dangerous working conditions for decades. Yet, profit between the global footwear industry earnings and the wages it pays to its subcontracted labor force continue (Ryan & During, 1998).

This chapter reflects lessons learned from case studies of Bandung (Indonesia) and Biñan (the Philippines) where the rudiments of shoemaking are learned at a young age to earn income as soon as possible. To set up a family shoe business, capital, equipment, lots of contacts, and good partners are necessary. Workers may not have the opportunity to set up their own workshop and thus remain piece-rate laborers for others. During peak production periods workers may labor around the clock as their paycheck depends on what they produce. Yet, the paycheck depends on orders, domestic market fluctuations, and increasingly globalization.

A global shoe production chain is diagramed in Figure 1. For example, in the case of exports to the United States, buying agents in the producing countries often are used by those U.S. companies that do not have a large representation abroad (Department of Labor, United States [DOL-US] 1997).

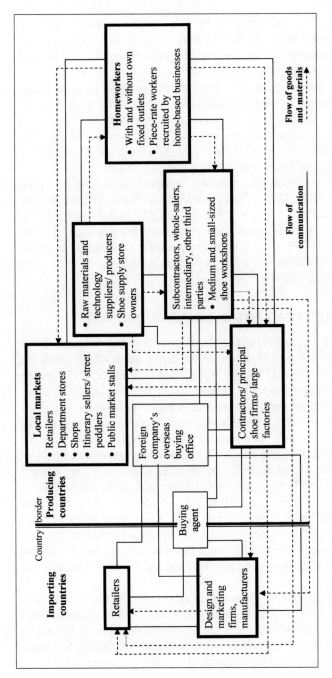

Figure 1. **Globalized and localized shoe production chain.** The scheme has been adapted by the author from these two literature sources: (i) The U.S. Department of Labor, the Bureau of International Labor Affairs, *By the sweat and toil of children (Vol. IV): Consumer labels and child labor*, 1997; (ii) The Department of Labor and Employment (DOLE), the Occupational Safety and Health Center, the Philippines: *Industry analysis of the footwear industry in Baranguay Dela Paz, Biñan, Laguna*, 2001. The sources adapted according to the interview findings of this research in Indonesia and the Philippines. Dotted lines illustrate the flow of goods and straight lines the flow of communication.

Overseas buying offices work directly for U.S. retailers, manufacturers, or design and marketing firms (DOL-US, 1997). Contractors—usually independently owned businesses—are responsible primarily for the actual footwear manufacturing (Occupational Safety and Health Center [OSHC], 2001a). These contractors operate their own factories and delegate parts manufacturing to subcontractors or other intermediaries who then use homeworkers' services—often on the basis of an unwritten agreement (OSHC, 2001a). The local retailers and department stores hire larger shoe manufacturers, or their subcontractors or intermediaries, or even on their own account workers for manufacturing orders in the domestic market (OSHC, 2001a).

In the U.S.-based athletic shoe industry, the shoe design and marketing remains primarily in the United States (McMichael, 2004). When considering domestic production, "made in the USA" usually means "assembled in the USA"—especially stitched shoe uppers that arrive from developing countries (Weisskoff, 1994). The labor of dyeing, cutting, stitching, assembling, packing, and transportation are often performed by women in developing countries (McMichael, 2004).

EMPLOYMENT AND GLOBAL PRODUCTION

During 1980-1995 global footwear output rose from $42 billion to $60.5 billion but this growth was regional. Asian output grew 424% while the Americas grew only 16% and Europe 10% (D'Mello, 2003). It is difficult to find reliable estimates for the size of informal sector workforce in the footwear industry. We can reach an approximation examining estimates of the total share of global informal labor. For Indonesia, the Asian Development Bank (ADB) estimated that in 2002, 64% of the country's total employment was in the informal economy (ADB, 2002). In 2003, informal labor represented 70% of the Philippines' total labor force (Department of Labor and Employment [DOLE], 2003). In 1997, the world employment estimate for the organized, formal footwear industry stood at 1.73 million, of which the Asian share was 36.6% (International Labour Office [ILO], 2000). This greatly underestimates the industry's total workforce when considering the close connection between the formal and informal sectors. Large manufacturers and retailers are known for their widespread subcontracting practices and the use of similar informal employment.

A 2000 ILO report, *Labour Practices in the Footwear, Leather, Textiles and Clothing Industries*, describes employment (ILO, 2000). Countries that employed large numbers of workers in the footwear industry were Indonesia, Mexico, Italy, Portugal, the United States and the Republic of Korea. Indonesia had a one-third share of world employment of women in footwear in 1995; the other five countries had a combined share of nearly 30% (ILO, 2000). The ILO determined that women's wages were universally lower than men's wages in the textile, clothing, and footwear sectors (ILO, 2000).

The glory years of U.S. shoe manufacturing—spearheaded by Massachusetts—occurred approximately from 1850 to 1950; production declined drastically during the 1960s. According to the American Apparel & Footwear Association (AAFA), in 1965, a total of 642.4 million shoe pairs were manufactured in the United States. In 2005, production was just a little bit more than 34 million pairs (AAFA, 2006). A total of 813 U.S. factories closed between 1967 and 2005. In 2005, there were an estimated 14,000 production employees who earned an average $11.50 an hour (AAFA, 2006).

From 1961 to 1991, the shoe imports share of the U.S. market rose from 6% to 72% (Weisskoff, 1994). Weisskoff traced two antitrust cases and suggested that they were at least part of the reason for the domestic production decline: (a) in 1953, the gigantic United Shoe Machinery Company's monopolistic leasing policy with royalty gains was obstructed; and (b) in 1963, the merger between the major shoe manufacturer (Kinney's) and retailer (Brown) was rejected to prevent market deprivation among other suppliers and sellers (Weisskoff, 1994). U.S. manufacturers no longer teamed up with machinery makers and chemical producers to develop new technologies. Instead, they rather relied on the government's protection and trade adjustment assistance (Weisskoff, 1994). Foreign producers entered with new materials and lower labor costs. For example, South Korea and Taiwan developed vinyl shoes; although less comfortable, they were cheaper. Retailers now started ordering directly from foreign manufacturers (Weisskoff, 1994).

Until 1980s, South Korea was a major athletic shoes exporter but democratic reforms, labor unrest, and economic development resulted in shoe workers' wages more than doubling in the 4 years before 1990 (Ryan & Durning, 1998). Over the next 3 years, employment in South Korea's shoe industry fell by 75% (Ryan & Durning, 1998). Shoe companies moved to China and Southeast Asia.

Domestically produced shoes now comprise merely 3% of the U.S. shoe market (AAFA, 2006). In 2006, China continued dominating the U.S. shoe markets with 85.4% of all imports; other major imports came to the United States from Brazil (3.5%), Viet Nam (2.9%), Indonesia (2.1%), as well as Italy, Thailand, and Mexico (AAFA, 2006).

Indonesia and the Philippines

Total footwear exports from Indonesia increased from US$1 million in 1980 to US$2.2 billion in 1996. In 1998, it was ranked as the second largest footwear employer in the world after China even though the country was severely hit by the financial crisis and exports decreased to $1.1 billion by the end of the year (ILO, 1999). By 2000, exports had risen to $2 billion but then dropped again to $1.1 billion by the end of 2002 (ILO, 1999; Laksmana, 2003). In 2002, over 40% of Indonesia's footwear exports went to U.S. markets, 33% to Europe, and the remaining share to African, Middle Eastern, and South American countries (Laksamana, 2003).

Bandung, the capital of West Java, has been the Indonesian footwear center since the early 1900s. Throughout the 1990s, production gradually has shifted nearer to Jakarta, particularly to Tangerang and East Java: the *Asia Times* reported that in 1998 international shoe brands constituted almost 94% of all Indonesian shoe exports—among them sports giants Nike, Adidas, and Reebok, which have preferred to contract local factories to manufacture their products (Guerin, 2002). Indeed, Indonesia is suffering from the relocation of multinational production, especially to Viet Nam and China; Indonesia's share of Nike's worldwide shoe production has declined from 38% to about 26% during 1996-2002 (Guerin, 2002). In 2002, Nike reduced Indonesian orders by an estimated 40% (Guerin, 2002).

Thousands of footwear workers participated in labor protests against giants like Nike and Reebok in 2002. The sneaker makers were blamed for increasing labor problems and decided to close down or relocate several factories. In mid 2002, Nike curtailed orders with its contractor, the PT Doson factory, placing 7,000 jobs at risk (International Confederation of Free Trade Unions [ICFTU], 2003a). The labor protest continued for several months and finally in November 2002, the Indonesian Textile, Garment, and Leather Worker Unions' Federation (SPTSK) won a deal for the jobless workers—PT Doson agreed to lend 500,000 rupiahs (about $58) to each worker (ICFTU, 2003b). In June 2003, about 5,000 PT Fortune Mate Indonesia shoe workers—predominantly women—protested for better conditions. The factory is located in Tambak Sawah, Rungkut, Surabaya (*The Jakarta Post,* 2003). The local labor union and the company failed to address workers' grievances, and the protesters blamed them for reduced allowances and demanded changes in the human resources department (*The Jakarta Post,* 2003).

For the Philippines, the footwear industry, especially footwear exports, has declined since the mid-1990s. Between 1991 and 1995, the industry grew at an annual rate of 11%, but it plummeted by 15% during 1996–2000; in 2000, the Philippines' footwear exports earned $76 million, the lowest level in the last 10 years (De Castro, 2001). According to the Department of Trade and Industry (DTI) data, footwear export value stood at $36.1 million in 2002 (DTI, 2003). In the Philippines, there has been a roiling debate about the dumping and smuggling of low-priced imported shoes into the country

(De Castro, 2001). Heated critiques indicate that such imports threaten domestic production. President Gloria Arroyo, among others, has asserted that the production process is not adequately modernized, whereas the Philippine Footwear Federation has pleaded with the government to cease the dumping and smuggling of footwear from China and Hong Kong and launched a *buy-Philippine-made-products* campaign (De Castro, 2001).

SHOEMAKING IN BANDUNG, INDONESIA[1]

The Nature of the Local Shoe Industry

Small-scale shoe producers mainly target the local market, and in Indonesia, they are found in several cities in the provinces of West and East Java (International Labour Office–International Programme on the Elimination of Child Labour [ILO-IPEC], 2004a). Bandung is one of them. Cibaduyut—an area located in southern Bandung—has been the city's shoemaking hub and is well-known for its home-based shoemaking involving all family members, including children. A skilled Cibaduyut shoemaker said:

> If the father can make shoes, the children can make shoes, and so do even the neighbors' children—(all) learn to make shoes. (Mr. Annan, skilled shoemaker/ organizer, interviewed in Bandung)

There are an estimated 1,500 skilled adult shoemakers in 200 businesses in Cibaduyut (Hakim, 2003). The craft is learned on average at 13–15 years of age, but sometimes even younger. The earlier children learn the shoemaking skills, the sooner they start earning income. Child shoemakers may carry out various tasks: cutting leather and sewing, grinding and gluing a sole to the upper part of the shoe, as well as selecting, cleaning, packing, and storing of goods (Hakim, 2003). *Tukangs*[2] start their careers as *keneks*.[3] Status as a helper at an adult age is considered shameful, so an apprenticeship is started in shoemaking as early as possible.

According to the 1999 ILO-IPEC Rapid Assessment study, there were 1,046 working children found in 436 workshops in Cibaduyut; these children constituted about 24% of the total shoe production workforce in the entire city of Bandung. Despite the encouraging decline, in 2003, there were still 256 child

---

[1] Profiles of Indonesian shoemakers interviewed are presented in Appendix I.

[2] *Tukang*, Indonesian term, means a skilled shoemaker.

[3] *Kenek*, Indonesian term, means helper or apprentice. In the shoe industry a *kenek* works normally for a *tukang*.

shoemakers found in Cibaduyut—most of them were boys, working approximately 9.5 hours a day, with an average 35,000 rupiah weekly wage (US$3.4[4]) (ILO-IPEC, 2004a). In February 2004, the number of child shoemakers had gone down to 58 (ILO-IPEC, 2004b).

Mr. Hiet, retired shoemaker and business owner, said that it was impossible to end child labor without the community opening a school for children to teach shoemaking and education related to the shoe industry. Such a school could be comparable to a senior high school, he said. Presently, when junior high school students complete their studies they start working. This institution would provide them with the opportunity to complete high school and learn shoemaking at the same time. Learning shoemaking as an apprentice after high school would be embarrassing:

> They don't have a special school for shoemaking. Until now we don't have it. NO skill sepatu[5] . . . So, children learn from experience. Experience from the tukang, from the earlier generation. (Mr. Hiet, retired shoemaker and business owner, interviewed in Bandung)

Dewi explained that a limit on children's education in footwear villages is tied to their parents' expectations for earnings. Sending children to work at an early age increased their earning potential over time. Parents believed that children who stayed in school would not earn as much as those who left early to acquire skills (Dewi, 2003). At the same time, she challenged the assumptions about a family's survival driving the decision to place children in work. Work as an income source and preservation of the "footwear culture" are both common social constructs in the community; boys especially are expected to know how to make footwear and money—the more the better—and not solely to overcome economic hardship but to procure goods and materials that may increase their social status (Dewi, 2003).

To set up a shoe workshop—or as Indonesians call it a *bengkel*—requires skills and capital. Often, if parents can provide enough money, space, and equipment, their children can run a *bengkel* immediately after high school. If not, they work for others, usually on small orders for individual custom made shoes. At this stage they rarely receive large purchase orders. On their path to establish a *bengkel,* they may start as intermediaries: buying and selling shoes.

Besides capital, a successful shoe business requires a network of contacts and good partners to work with. Shoemakers (*tukangs*) who are known to be very skillful may be lucky enough to receive orders directly from shops,

---

[4]Currency rate of September 23, 2005: 1US$ = 10,225 Indonesian rupiah.
[5]Sepatu is the Indonesian language word for "a shoe."

not only from brokers. Shop owners ask *tukangs* to produce a certain style of shoes and pay in advance for raw material. The businesses recruit other *tukangs*[6] when orders reach about 200 pairs a week. Not everyone wants to become a business owner because good *tukangs* are highly respected among businesses that produce for well-known and special brands. Recruiters are looking for *tukangs;* in Cibaduyut, 300,000 rupiahs (about $36)[7] can be paid to a *tukang* just to transfer him from one *bengkel* to another.

Almost every shoemaker I interviewed affirmed that continuous orders and cash payments are the best part of shoemaking. Cash covers the business and household costs as well as the children's school expenses. Ms. Dessy mentioned that owning a shoe brand brings more stable business. Mr. Saleh mentioned that the intriguing part of his business was the challenge when shoe styles changed; especially for girls' and women's shoes, models change frequently.

In Cibadudyt, *bengkel* owners often buy uppers, soles, leather, glues, and other raw materials from retail shops. There are special importers and distributors for uppers and for bottoms. Mr. Iman's customer was the army, which supplied standardized sole parts. Some others received their bottoms from a factory in Bogor and leather from a tannery in Tangerang (near Jakarta). Shoemakers working for one principal company often received raw materials from that company with the costs deducted after production was completed.

Customers

End customers include shops, local department stores, open-air market stalls, and street peddlers. Shoemakers who have their products displayed on the main street may eventually receive direct orders. Shops in Cianjur, 60 kilometers from Cibaduyut, are also Cibadut shoemakers' customers. Bandung customers come from Dalem Kaum street where the traditional shopping centers are located. Orders come from the capital Jakarta where many wholesalers are located. Numerous wholesalers have marketing staff that travel around Indonesia. Some shoe producers also travel. One *bengkel* owner described how he traveled with shoe samples and took orders from shops.

Producers also enter agreements with wholesalers who distribute shoes throughout Indonesia. They place orders after reviewing the shoemakers' samples. A normal order is usually about 20 pairs for one style. The wholesaler

[6]Generally, recruitment means that *tukangs* come to work in the workshop premises of the owner as piece-rate workers. Small home-based workshop owners are normally not allowed to subcontract to outsiders.

[7]Currency rate as of 22 November 2003. $1 US = 8,517.50 Indonesian rupiah.

may show the samples to a retailer or department store. Smaller *bengkels*, with a capacity of 20 pairs a week, usually seek out their customers. Some Cibaduyut *bengkel* owners and shoemakers I interviewed knew that their managers exported shoes to countries like Malaysia, Nigeria, and Saudi Arabia. Someone suspected the United States to be a destination. For most producers in the Cibaduyut shoe manufacturing community, cash flow is a major concern. When they experience cash flow delays, they often start selling their personal assets. Liquidation is not uncommon. For example, say a business owner couple just sold their leather. If their cash flow is disrupted, sometimes businesses sell raw material goods to other *tukangs at* a lower price than the one at which they acquired the materials. That is why it is possible to find shoes that are of the same quality and style selling at different prices.

For big department stores, order deadlines are strict. If a shipment is late, the principal company may suffer a 5% payment deduction. Quality control is strict and standards must be followed. Products are rejected and returned, if for example, the shoes are not clean enough. In some bigger factories, if a worker makes a mistake, the cost of the shoe is deducted from wages.

Profit margins for shoe producers are small. If one shop sells a pair of shoes for 50,000 rupiahs, another will sell them for 30,000 a pair. When expenses are deducted, the profit margin may be just 1,000 rupiahs per pair (about 12 cents). If shoemakers do not receive cash, the business is at risk. A common practice in Cibaduyut is for an order to be paid 50% in cash and 50% by check. When money is needed for raw materials, the check can be used but at a 20% lower value. If the check value is not decreased, shops will simply increase the product's price. After a check has circulated around Cibaduyut, it has to be cashed and the procedure becomes a complicated one. Shoemakers sometimes must find the person who issued it. If they manage to find the person, they may receive another check which can be cashed 1 to 2 months later. Checks must be accepted, otherwise customers go elsewhere.

How Much Do Shoemakers Earn in Bandung?

Skilled shoemakers were usually paid weekly. A small *bengkel* (one to three workers) could earn 10 to 15 million rupiahs (about US$1,200–US$1,800) a week. Workers' wages range from 100,000 rupiahs ($12) to 200,000 rupiahs ($24) a week. Earnings depend on output and that depends on orders. On average, skilled shoemakers earn $4 a day. Skilled shoemakers who produced custom-made boots earn $21–$24 a week. A business owner explained that during a good peak season period, the profit margin was about 50,000 rupiahs every 20 pairs of shoes. In a week he could produce 200 pairs and earn about 500,000 rupiahs ($59). He could afford to send his children to school.

SHOEMAKING IN MARIKINA AND IN BIÑAN, THE PHILIPPINES

Marikina

Although Laguna province (where Biñan is located and which will be the focus of this study) has the highest number of shoe producers, the country's shoe capital is considered to be Marikina (50 kilometers from Manila). With 600 registered companies (Vitug, 2001), Marikina's shoe manufacturing is more formal and mechanized than Biñan's, and most shoes are destined for export or big shopping malls. But Marikina's shoe industry in not yet sufficiently modernized to compete in global markets (Vitug, 2001). *Newsweek International* reported that Marikina's footwear industry has been vital to the Philippines economy for decades. In the mid-1980s, the Philippines was a big shoe exporter to the United States and other countries (The Manila Standard, 2003). But this is no longer the case, although some people I talked to believe that over 2001-2002 Marikina's shoe industry has increased its exports to Italy and the United States. In August 2003, 78 companies formed a universal firm to boost the city's shoe industry. The new corporation was called *Marquina* and plans to make shoes that carry the *Marquina* name (The Manila Standard, 2003).

Biñan

Biñan is divided into 24 Baranguays (i.e., districts) and has an estimated population about 208,000. Footwear manufacturing companies are concentrated in three Baranguays: Malaban (21%); Dela Paz (17%); and Calabuso (13%) (OSHC, 2001a).

Dela Paz specializes in the production of children's shoes, step-ins, and women's sandals and Malaban specializes in men's shoes and more expensive women's shoes (OSHC, 2001a). In 1999, there were 151 registered footwear manufacturers in Biñan (OSHC, 2001a), but this figure represents a fraction of the true number of firms there. In Biñan, IPEC's monitors visited 1,204 shoe workshops and determined that 617 of them employed close to 2,000 children (OSHC, 2001b, 2002). Biñan's footwear production is almost all home-based and mechanized production is almost non-existent (OSHC, 2001a). Most of the people I talked to expressed concern over the weakening of footwear production. Shoes are almost exclusively for the domestic market and a large share of them are sold at small public markets (OSHC, 2001a). Concerns about the negative effects of globalization are legitimate; global competition could easily swallow up the region's home-based producers.

The Nature of the Local Shoe Industry [8]

The Philippine Occupational Safety and Health Center's (OSH Center) footwear study identified four key segments of the local industry: (a) buyers, namely: end-customers and consumers (market shoppers), market stallholders who order shoes directly from footwear workers and then sell to shoppers, large institutional buyers who buy through agents and subcontractors/managers; (b) raw material stores which are mostly owned by Filipino-Chinese; (c) subcontractors who are locally called "managers." I use the terms subcontractor and manager interchangeably; and (d) footwear manufacturers who produce mostly for subcontractors (or sometimes for the end-customer) are called suppliers locally. The OSH Center study revealed that market bargaining power is directly equated to the size of shoe purchases. Large buyers, like Shoe Mart, exercise immense control over producers due to the volume of their orders. Some storeowners and subcontractors can make considerable profits. It is the shoe manufacturers who have little leverage because they exist in large numbers and lack technology capital.

Typically, shoe manufacturers design samples that subcontractors/managers show to potential customers. It is unclear whether the manager, the shoe producer, or the store owns the design. But, shoemakers' rights are rarely respected and they usually do not receive any payment for their designs and samples. When stores accept a sample, they provide the subcontractors/ managers with an order specifying the volume to be manufactured, cost paid, and delivery date. The delivery time must be met or the end customer may cancel the order. Products that do not meet a customer's quality standards can also be rejected and returned without compensation.

Managers sometimes serve as exclusive material suppliers. Producers may also be required to receive their raw materials only from a specific storeowner. Materials are often bought on credit, with the interest charged ranging from 10 to 15%. Occasionally, subcontractors/managers provide an advance payment to the producer using a post-dated check. While some producers may want to become managers, it is difficult to overcome a lack of capital, few contacts, a small supply network, and the upfront costs associated with doing business with institutional buyers. Very few home-based shoemakers hire permanent workers. Instead they recruit temporary help on a piece-rate basis when orders warrant it. For example, to complete an order of 100 dozen pairs of sandals in one month, a manufacturer might

---

[8] This whole subsection is based on information from *Industry Analysis of the Footwear Industry in Baranguay Dela Paz, Biñan, Laguna* by the Occupational Safety and Health Center of the Philippines.

hire three piece-rate workers.[9] Subcontractors sell sandals for roughly 160 pesos,[10] a bit less than $3 a pair. About 38% of this goes to the subcontractor, 56% to cover raw materials and labor costs, leaving 6% for the household shoe producer.

Footwear manufacturers purchase their raw materials at designated stores with the price deducted from the value of the purchase order. Shoe manufacturers often do not know what the subcontractor/manager paid for materials. And, when a cash advance is requested, deception may occur. Raw material prices may be increased or interest raised. Finished products are transported to customers by managers.

Dilemma of Imported Shoes

Shoe producers used to consider shoemaking a good source of livelihood. But, like many others, the representative of the local footwear manufacturing association believed that Biñan's shoe industry was weakening. Shoe producers were seeking alternative jobs like sea fishing. Many producers found it difficult to find markets because imported shoes were flowing into the region. As a result of increased imports, Biñan shoe manufacturers decided to organize. The representative's sources suggested that the country imported shoe products worth billions of pesos in 1997. By 2001, the figure had not changed for the better. A concern was whether additional products entered the country illegally. Most of the imported shoes originated from China, and were much cheaper than domestic products. The raw material used in local production was expensive and local producers paid taxes. The representative suggested that the Undersecretary of the Department of Technology and Industry (DTI) determine on how Filipinos might produce their own local raw materials. Small producers also expressed their concerns about imported shoes to Gloria Arroyo, the president of the country, and explained how imports threatened their livelihood. President Arroyo indicated that footwear producers needed to modernize to cut their production costs (De Castro, 2001). When asked whether he was optimistic about the revival of the footwear sector, the representative responded:

> Since I have experience in preparing legislations and identifying problems affecting people, I believe I could do so much for the welfare of our manufacturers and workers in the footwear industry. But since

[9]Piece-rate workers are often outsiders, not necessarily part of the immediate family or household members.

[10]Currency rate on 22 November 2003: $1 US = 55.56 Philippines pesos.

our major problem now is on the importation of footwear products, we need to deal with this problem first. My second priority is the improvement of technology. The third concern is to go down to the different Baranguays (villages) to conduct orientations and trainings with shoe manufacturers, with the help of the Occupational Safety and Health Center. (Representative of the local footwear manufacturing association, interviewed in Biñan)

To revive the Philippine shoe sector, one legislature introduced a bill (House Bill 5566) to promote the development of the footwear, leather, and tannery industries (Congress of the Philippines, 2001). The bill was approved by the President on April 15, 2004 (Congress of the Philippines, 2004).

How Much Do Shoemakers Earn in Biñan?

As for wages, workers earned $1.80–2.70 a day, a very small amount, no matter how low living costs were. Families with several children could not afford to send them to school beyond the elementary level. Workers in one large factory earned a basic salary of $4 a day. Income for subcontractors, shoe producers, and raw material suppliers depended on orders from retailers, large institutional buyers, and other end-customers. Few orders were placed during the "lean months" of July, August, and September. The peak manufacturing season normally lasted from October until December.

Many shoe producers I interviewed[11] noted that orders remained down throughout 2002. In Biñan, when whole families were involved in production, income was not calculated for individual family members. An analysis carried out by the OSH Center revealed that an order worth of $1,800 might result in a profit of $90–180. Outside piece-rate workers' wages would be deducted from this, leaving very little family profit (OSHC, 2001a).

Mr. and Mrs. Martinez said that they could produce from 9 to 12 dozen pairs of shoes a week. Thirty dozen pairs of shoes in a 3-week to 1-month period brought in 3,000 pesos—which is net of the cost of materials. Mrs. John said that her family were lucky if something was left after they paid for raw materials.

For the work I am doing right now, I was told that the manager will pay 70 pesos only after I was given a cash advance. We thought that we will be paid 90 to 100 pesos per pair. There is really no income, we

[11] Profiles of shoemakers presented in Appendix I.

do not know what to do in this business. It is really better to have
your own capital. (Mrs. John, a homeworker, interviewed in Biñan)

Mrs. John further explained that during slowdowns they took other jobs. She
worked as a sewer and her husband as a driver. The income was needed to raise
four children. In 2001, they took out a micro-loan but could not pay it back.
In August 2002, an order came but the couple waited months for special
raw materials to arrive from Hong Kong. While they waited, she was earning
income catering food. Mr. and Mrs. Martinez produced an average of 20 dozen
pairs of shoes each month. Average monthly earnings were $54. Mr. Carino,
another home business owner, earned $9–11 a week.

Mr. and Mrs. Eno's (subcontractor family) earnings fluctuated during the
year. Sales were good during the Christmas season, graduation months, and the
opening of school. Sales did not fall below $5,400 for December. During the
graduation months of March and April sales were $3,600–4,500 a month.
During the school openings in June sales could reach $2,700. Mr. and Mrs. Eno
set up the business in 1983 with a loan from a raw material supplier. Keeping
the creditor's trust was crucial. Mrs. Lane, subcontractor/operation manager,
earned about $22 a week for about 50 dozen pairs of shoes. Mr. Anton, the
owner of a larger business/subcontractor, mentioned that if his shoemakers
worked very hard, they could earn $63 in six days. His profit was about 8%
of the production price. The check payments were a problem for producers.
Mr. Henry noted that if he asked for a $36 cash advance from a manager, he
received a check. If it was exchanged with a raw material supplier, deduc-
tions were made. Such checks are not cashed in the banks because they are
post-dated. Hence, producers exchange them for cash and raw materials at a
lower value. Producers might also be paid with a post-dated check after they
have completed the entire shoe production order.

CONCLUSION

Shoemakers in both countries feel that receiving large orders from
customers is the best part of the business. But, the long periods without orders
are typical and during such periods many family-based owners go to work for
larger operators as piece-rate workers. In both countries, footwear production
is considered physically less strenuous than many other occupations. New
shoe designs kept producers' work interesting as did meeting people while
delivering products. All in all, shoemakers felt pride for their work and hazards
addressed in the next chapter will not stop them producing fotwear.

APPENDIX I
Profiles of Interviewed Shoemakers and Producers[a]
in Indonesia and the Philippines

Bandung, Indonesia	
Person interviewed	**Background description**
1. Mr. and Mrs. Dahn – shoemakers and business owners	Married couple, both the husband and wife present and active in the interview. Mr. Dahn (38) started the business after senior high school.
2. Mr. Hiet – retired shoemaker and business owner	Mr. Hiet (61), "retired" from day-to-day shoe manufacturing, is the leader of an institution to empower the community. He has been making shoes his entire life. His grandfather taught him shoemaking and his father taught him sewing skills; thus, he became both a shoemaker and a dress-maker. Since 1975, Mr. Hiet worked in a boutique making dresses. In 1982, he got involved in the shoe industry by selling and marketing the shoes made by his relatives. Two of his children make shoes. Now, his children take care of the business management but he helps them. They own two shoe workshops: one with six workers, and the other one with three workers.
3. Mrs. Dessy – female business manager	Mrs. Dessy (43) runs a family-based shoe business which she inherited from her parents. The business is in her name, but every family member is involved in its management. Her husband comes from Cibaduyut; he is a *tukang* and his parents also owned a *bengkel.* Both of them have been in the shoe industry for more than 20 years. The husband designs the shoe models and their two children help them. Their son takes care of the delivery. The daughter is in charge of marketing and accounting; while marketing, she goes to different shops with footwear samples and takes orders. Besides the *bengkel* house, the family has a house a little farther away, but only her children live there now. Mrs. Dessy rarely leaves the *bengkel;* during a busy period she stays there overnight, sometimes working until the morning. In addition to the family members, there are 11 other workers in the *bengkel.*

[a]Names of all shoemakers and producers have been changed.

APPENDIX I
(Cont'd.)

Bandung, Indonesia

Person interviewed	Background description
4. Mr. Hakim – custom-made boots producer	Mr. Hakim produces custom-made boots and his wife participates in the business management. They have a daughter. A special last is prepared for the customer to fit the shoes nicely to the customer's feet. His customers included many musicians and artists. He is not affiliated with any employers' or other organizations. Besides the *bengkel,* Mr. Hakim owns a shop in Bandung where his products are sold.
5. Mr. Ari – skilled shoemaker (*tukang*)	Mr. Ari (36) is a skilled shoemaker (*tukang*). He is married and has three children. Mr. Ari produces sandals. He has been involved in shoe manufacturing work for about 20 years. At the beginning, he wanted to continue his studies, but his parents could not afford it, so he decided to work as a shoemaker. He started as an employee and eventually set up his own business. If the order is a large one, he employs four people to make the uppers and two more to assemble; otherwise, he produces the shoes himself. His wife helps him with packing and cleaning. At the time of the interview, he had not received any orders for a month, even though it was a peak production season.
6. Mr. Saleh – skilled shoemaker/ business owner	Mr. Saleh (36) is a business owner. He is married and has two daughters. He owns a shoe workshop to produce for a rather well-known brand. He started working as a shoe producer in 1984, but quit six years later and got involved then in the production of rattan furniture and *nata de coco.*[b] Ten years later, in 2000, he decided to go back to the business. Mr. Saleh was also an athlete (a badminton coach), and that position helped him to make contacts with Chinese businessmen—one of whom took him to see the factory of a well-known brand. The factory manager agreed on an initial small order of 300 pairs for two weeks. Now, he produces 300 pairs in one to two days which is considered a big capacity. The *bengkel* is outside of his living space, where his *tukangs* work. Everything should be produced in the

APPENDIX I
(Cont'd.)

Bandung, Indonesia

Person interviewed	Background description
	bengkel—subcontracting would break his relationship with the principal. At the beginning, the factory manager was hesitant to give him orders, so he and his friend had to convince the other Chinese directors that he produced alone and would not subcontract.
7. Mr. Annan – skilled shoemaker/ organizer	Mr. Annan (43) is a *tukang*. He is married and has two children. Mr. Annan has been producing shoes for 24 years. Now, he is the chief of the *Tukang's* association, and for the last two years he has been an elected village cluster chief. Twenty-four years ago, he came the the area outside of Cibaduyut and decided to work as a shoe worker. His home was 60 kilometers away and daily commuting was impossible. He lived with his employer. Later, he set up his own *bengkel* with the support of his wife. At that time, the only available job for him was making shoes. He started as an apprentice and the *bengkel* owner taught him the shoemaking craft. He worked as a *tukang* for seven years. At the time of the interview, he did not produce shoes but was active in the *Tukang's* association.
8. Mr. Iman – business owner	Mr. Iman (32) is married and has 3 children. Has been in the business since 1990 (12 years).
9. Mr. Abdul – business owner	Mr. Abdul (46) started his business in 1978. 1981–1984 he worked for other business owners. In 1985, he re-started his own business.
10. Mr. Eni – shoemaker/business owner	Mr. Eni (63), married, and has 10 children.
11. Mr. Sri – piece-rate worker	Mr. Sri (24) is unmarried. He makes shoe uppers. He started working at the age of 16.

[b]Dessert made of coconuts.

APPENDIX I
(Cont'd.)

Biñan, The Philippines

Person interviewed	Background description
1. Mr. Henry – piece-rate worker	A 61-year old, married, piece-rate worker, and has five children. Mr. Henry has been manufacturing shoes for 25 years. He does not own his own business but works for other shoe workshops. He mentioned that earning income in Biñan was easy if one knew how to make women's shoes or slippers.
2. Mr. and Mrs. Francis – shoemakers and business owners	Mr. Francis (41) and Mrs. Francis (38) have been manufacturing shoes in their own workshop for ten years. They have two children. The children formerly helped the family in shoe production. Both Mr. and Mrs. Francis participated in the interview.
3. Mrs. John	In the Johns' family, Mrs. John participated in the interview. Mrs. John prepares upper parts, cleans the finished shoes, and brings the finished products to the subcontractor. At the time of the interview, little work was being offered. The family has lived in Biñan's Baranguay Dela Paz for almost four years because the husband inherited the house from his parents. Before that, they had lived in the Baranguay Malaban and owned a shoe business for two years. During production slowdown, she worked for other shoe workshops as a sewer. Mr. John is a driver.
4. Mr. and Mrs. Martinez	Mr. and Mrs. Martinez have had their home-based shoe manufacturing business for 15 years. Only Mrs. Martinez participated in the interview. Both are in their early 50s. Mrs. Martinez previously worked for other shoe workshops. Her husband was in his second year in high school when he learned shoemaking; he quit the school at the age of 15. Now, they manufacture mainly children's sandals.
5. Mr. Carino – home-business owner	A home-business owner, Mr. Carino, manufactures sandals and ladies' shoes. At the time of the interview, there were three male and two female piece-rate workers in his workshop. He started the work as a young boy, about at the age of 10, by helping his father lining upper parts, applying adhesives, and stitching. He inherited the business from his parents.

APPENDIX I
(Cont'd.)

Biñan, The Philippines

Person interviewed	Background description
6. Mr. Lopez – a piece-rate worker	A male employee in Mr. Carino's workshop.
7. Mr. and Mrs. Eno – a subcontractor family	Mr. and Mrs. Eno, married since 1971, started their subcontracting business in 1983. From 1973 to 1983, they had a home-based shoe workshop wherein they produced for other subcontractors. At the time of the interview, they had 25 shoe workshops around the area suppling footwear products for them. Mrs. Eno said that they did not charge interest on their cash advances and raw materials—the reason why shoe workshops are willing to supply for them. Their children help manage the business.
8. Mrs. Lane – subcontractor/ operation manager	Mrs. Lane (39) is married and has three children. She started the subcontracting business with her sister-in-law as a shoe producer. Both call themselves subcontractors, but she considers her sister-in-law the main manager and herself the operation manager. She used to be a high school teacher and got involved in the shoe business in 1993 as a shoemaker—not as a manager. Mrs. Lane made more money in the shoe business than as a teacher. However, she misses teaching and plans to go back to it when shoe orders plummet. At the time of the interview, they had at least 30 shoe workshops supplying footwear products to them in addition to their own production.
9. Representative of the local footwear manufacturing association	Representative of the local footwear manufacturing association was selected to lead the Biñan organization because of his service in the local government and experience in the local footwear industry. He was nine years old when he started working in his family's shoe business. He prepared shoeboxes, ground soles, made hardboard for the bottom of the molded head of the shoes, and prepared in-soles. As a teenager, he knew how to make a whole shoe, slipper, or sandal. There were

APPENDIX I
(Cont'd.)

Biñan, The Philippines

Person interviewed	Background description
	even times when his mother asked him and his siblings not to go to school because an order had to be finished. During Saturdays, Sundays, and after school hours, he made shoes and carried out other tasks.
10. Mr. Smith – the community organizer	The community organizer, Mr. Smith, was a footwear operator for 11 years before he became a child labor monitor with the ILO-IPEC Team and organizer at the local non-government organization in Biñan. During his childhood, he was a leader of a religious group, youth organizer, and sacristan (the one who assists the priest during celebration of mass).
11. Mr. Anton – the owner of a larger shoe business/ subcontractor	The owner of a larger shoe business—Mr. Anton (43) is married, and has two children. His father taught him how to make shoes when he was 13. During his high school years, he dyed slippers at their family shoe workshop whenever there were products to be finished. He also worked for their neighbor's shoe workshop when his father's business declined. He worked at paper mill production from 1983 until 1996; nonetheless, he started his shoe business in 1990 by manufacturing three or four design pairs at a time. After a while, customers were looking for more designs and he started getting orders for dozens of pairs. At the time of the interview, about 60 people worked for him.

BIBLIOGRAPHY

American Apparel & Footwear Association. (2006). *ShoeStats 2006* (pp. i-vi). Arlington, Virginia. Retrieved at:
http://www.apparelandfootwear.org/UserFiles/File/Statistics/shoestats2006.pdf

Asian Development Bank (ADB). (2002). *Country economic review: Indonesia* (p. 5). Manila: ADB. Retrieved at:
http://www.adb.org/Documents/CERs/INO/2003/default.asp

Congress of the Philippines. (2001). 12th Congress, First Regular Session. Explanatory note by representative Del R. de Guzman on House Bill 3950 (Footwear, Leather, and Tannery Industries Development Act).

Congress of the Philippines. (2004). An act promoting the development of the footwear, leather goods and tannery industries, providing incentives therefor and for other purposes. Republic Act No. 9290. Retrieved at:
http://www.congress.gov.ph/download/RA02290.pdf

D'Mello, B. (2003). Reebok and the global footwear sweatshop. *Monthly Review, 54*(9). Retrieved at: http://www.monthlyreview.org/

De Castro, I. (2001). Your left shoe is from China. *Newsbreak, 1*(32).

Department of Labor, United States (DOL-US). (1997). *By the sweat and toil of children (Vol. IV). Consumer labels and child labor* (p. 65). The Bureau of International Labor Affairs. Retrieved at:
http://www.dol.gov/ilab/media/reports/iclp/sweat4/leather.htm

Department of Trade and Industry (DTI). (2003). *Summary of Philippine merchandise exports to all countries by major product grouping during 2003-2002.* Retrieved at: http://tradelinephil.dti.gov.ph/betp/statcod3.sumprod

Dewi, S. E. (2003). *Community values, education and work: Child labor in Indonesia— The case of the household footwear sector in Cibaduyut and Cangkuang Kulon, Bandung.* Masters thesis, The University of Massachusetts Lowell.

Guerin, B. (2002). Weak footing for Indonesia's shoe industry. *Asia Times.* Retrieved November 28: http://www.atimes.com/atimes/Southeast_Asia/DK28Ae02.html

Hakim, A. (2003). *The improvement of the safety and health of workers as an avenue into eliminating child labour in the informal footwear sector.* The paper presented at the National Occupational Safety and Health Conference, in Jakarta, January 13, 2003.

International Confederation of Free Trade Unions (ICFTU). (2003a). *Indonesia: Annual survey of violations of trade union rights.* Retrieved at: http://www.icftu.org/

International Confederation of Free Trade Unions (ICFTU). (2003b). *Internationally recognized core labour standards in Indonesia.* Report for the WTO General Council review of trade policies of Indonesia. ICFTU, Geneva. Retrieved at: http://www.icftu.org/

International Labour Office (ILO). (2000). *Labour practices in the footwear, leather, textiles and clothing industries.* Report for discussion at the tripartite meeting. Sectoral Activities Department. ILO, Geneva, pp. 27, 48.

International Labour Office–International Programme on the Elimination of Child Labour (ILO-IPEC). (2004a). *Child labour in the informal footwear sector in West Java: A rapid assessment.* International Labour Organization, Jakarta.

International Labour Office–International Programme on the Elimination of Child Labour (ILO-IPEC). (2004b). *Progress report to the US-DOL on the project of combating child labour in the Indonesian footwear sector, September 2003–March 2004.* International Labour Organization, Jakarta.

Laksamana. (2002). Private sector: Gloom in shoes. *The Politics and Economics Portal.*

McMichael P. (2004). *Development and social change: A global perspective* (3rd ed.; pp. xxx-xxxii). Thousand Oaks, CA: Pine Forge Press.

National Agency for Export Development. (2003). *Europe lifts the antidumping duty on Indonesian footwear.* The Department of Trade and Industry, Indonesia. Retrieved at: http://www.nafed.go.id/

Occupational Safety and Health Center, the Philippines (OSHC). (2001a). *Industry analysis of the footwear industry in Baranguay Dela Paz, Biñan, Laguna.* The Department of Labor and Employment (DOLE), the Philippines.

Occupational Safety and Health Center, the Philippines (OSHC). (2001b). *Manual on training of trainers on occupational safety and health approach for child labor in the footwear industry.* The Department of Labor and Employment (DOLE), the Philippines.

Occupational Safety and Health Center (OSHC). (2002). *Hope for the children of Biñan: A community wakes up to protect the younger generation.* A video documentary. Department of Labor and Employment (DOLE), the Philippines.

Ryan, B., & Durning, A. (1998). The story of a shoe. *WorldWatch,* pp. 29-31. Retrieved at: http://www.worldwatch.org/system/files/EP112C.pdf

The Jakarta Post. (2003). *5,000 shoe workers protest for better pay.* June 9, 2003.

The Manila Standard. (2003). Footnote: 78 Marikina shoemakers link up.

United Nations Development Programme (UNDP). (2003). *Human development report. Millennium development goals: A compact among nations to end human poverty.* New York: Oxford University Press (for the UNDP). Retrieved at: http://hdr.undp.org/en/reports/global/hdr2003/

Vitug, M. D. (2001). Shoe industry's slow death. *Newsweek International, 138*(10), p. 34.

Weisskoff, R. (1994). The decline of the US footwear industry and the expected impact of a free trade agreement between Colombia and the United States. *North American Journal of Economy & Finance, 5*(1), 55-78.

CHAPTER 2

❦

Shoemaking and its Hazards

ORGANIC SOLVENT AND DUST
EXPOSURES WORLDWIDE

There are many common hazards in shoemaking throughout the world. Various organic solvents are found in footwear chemicals: glues, primers, cleaning agents. A study by the Maquila Solidarity Network determined that a chronic problem observed by shoe factory monitors is the lack of adequate worker protection when handling glues, primers, degreasers, and cleaners (Thomas, 1998). Toluene is a common solvent—but not the only solvent—used in these chemicals. The storage of toxic and flammable chemicals constitutes not only a health hazard but a fire and explosion hazard which also endangers neighboring residences. In May 2002, fire killed 44 shoe manufacturing workers in the city of Agra, India (International Textile, Garment and Leather Workers' Federation [ITGLF], 2001). The cause of the fire was likely a short circuit in an adhesive drums storeroom. The drums exploded and the flames spread to the factory premises (ITGLF, 2001).

Mayan, Pires, Neves, and Capela (1999) conducted a solvent exposure study in 100 shoe factories in northern Portugal which employed 4,615 workers, predominantly women (Mayan et al., 1999). Their air sample results indicated 20 different organic compounds; the most common were n-hexane, toluene, acetone (present in more than 85% of the studied factories) and considerable amounts of ethyl acetate (>65%), methyl-ethyl-ketone (MEK) (>50%), and dichloromethane (>30%). More than half of the factories had hazardous solvent exposure levels, in particular at gluing, waxing, and polishing stations (Mayan et al., 1999).

Nervous System Effects

Epidemiological studies suggest an association of long-term solvent exposure with damage to the central nervous system. Studies by Nijem, Kristensen, Thorud, Al-Khatib, Takrori, and Bjertness, indicated that shoe industry workers with chronic organic solvent exposures exhibited neurological abnormalities, poorer neurobehavioral performance, impaired memory, and concentration problems (Nijem et al., 1998). Shoe workers in Hebron City were exposed to dichloromethane in cleaning work, acetone, n-hexane, toluene, and MEK in adhesive applications, toluene in polishing, diisocyanate in plastic sole curing, and polyvinyl chloride (PVC) fumes in molding (Nijem et al., 1998). Workers' self-reports revealed both increased neuropsychiatric effects and mucous membrane irritation (Nijem et al., 1998). Lee and colleagues administered a neurobehavioral Core Test Battery to 40 Korean shoe manufacturing workers who were exposed to a mixture of solvents, including toluene, MEK, n-hexane, cyclohexane, dichloroethylene, benzene, and xylene. The group with higher exposures had significantly poorer performance than the reference group (Lee, Park, Kim, Lee, Kim, & Kang, 1998). Among others, a number of Italian and Spanish researchers have reported an association between polyneuropathy and n-hexane as well as n-heptane exposures (Bovenzi, Fiorito, & Patussi, 1990; Cardona et al., 1993; Passero et al., 1983; Valentini et al., 1994).

Paul Blanc described implementation of hexane as a glue solvent to replace benzene. Quickly, it became clear that hexane exposure brought its own health hazards. At the end of 1960s, notices published in Japan described an abnormal outbreak of a neurological disorder: the victims suffered from loss of both sensation and muscle strength, particularly in the arms (Blanc, 2007). The largest outbreak had claimed 93 victims—from children to elderly—all of them living in a small region dominated by a shoe "cottage" industry:

> Typical of inhabitants of this area, it had been their conventional means of livelihood to make sandals or slippers. In recent years, utilization of synthetic resins to this household industry has occurred and many kinds of organic solvents have been used as a rubber paste base . . . they have engaged in the work more than 8 hrs a day in narrow, badly ventilated dwellings where vapor of the volatile solvent filled the rooms. (Blanc, 2007)

Soon, other countries published similar reports, and by the 1970s, the illness had a name: *shoemaker's polyneuropathy* (Blanc, 2007). Bill Bowerman—the Nike cofounder and inventor—is perhaps one of the most well-known victim of shoemaker's polyneuropathy. He used to work in a small space with a hexane-based glue when developing shoe prototypes in his home (Blanc, 2007).

Respiratory System Effects

The ILO has studied chemical risks in various small- and medium-sized enterprises (Watfa, Awan, & Goodson, 1998). In shoemaking, in addition to exposures to adhesives, the ILO found exposures to hexane for cleaning leather and white spirit or gasoline for removing excess glue and hand cleaning. The ILO investigators also found that leather and rubber dusts inhaled by workers sometimes contain adhesive and other unevaporated solvent residues.

In 1977, Zuskin and colleagues studied respiratory effects from shoe manufacturing in 376 female workers—mostly non-smokers—in a Croatian factory (Zuskin, Mustajbegovic, Schachter, Doko-Jelinic, & Bradic, 1997). Environmental air measurements detected solvents and dusts such as xylenol, toluene, acetone, ethylacetate, ethanol, benzene, butanol, MEK, along with fur dust and synthetic fibers. Higher prevalences of both chronic and acute respiratory symptoms were recorded in exposed workers than in the control group, including chest tightness, dyspnea, rhinitis, and nose and throat irritation. All lung function capacity tests showed reduced values for exposed workers (Zuskin et al., 1997). Researchers concluded that shoe manufacturing work could be responsible for the development of acute and chronic respiratory impairment (Zuskin et al., 1997).

Potential Carcinogens?

In 1987, the International Agency for Research on Cancer (IARC) documented cancer studies related to footwear manufacturing and repair. The studies indicated a strong association between leather dust exposure and nasal cancer (nasal adenocarcinomas) (IARC, 1987). Footwear workers exposed to benzene have been widely documented as suffering leukemia and anemia (Constatini, Quinn, Consonni, & Zappa, 2003; IARC, 1987; Ward, Burnett, Ruder, & Davis-King, 1997). In the United States, epidemiological studies conducted in the 1980s found that footwear industry work was associated with bladder cancer and digestive system cancers. No strong relation to nasal cancers was demonstrated (Walrath, Decoufle, & Thomas, 1987). A decade later, Fu, Demers, Constantini, Winter, Colin, Kogevinas, et al. (1996) examined the cancer risk among more than 4,000 English and 2,000 Italian shoemakers. Their results indicated associations between leather dust exposure and nasal cancer, as well as benzene exposure and leukemia. They suggested that the risk of other cancers, like stomach and bladder, multiple myeloma, and non-Hodgkin's lymphoma, may increase among workers exposed to glue solvents (Fu et al., 1996).

Pitarque and colleagues investigated potential carcinogenic signs of toluene and other organic solvent mixtures by evaluating the blood leukocyte DNA damage in 34 female shoe workers in two Bulgarian shoe factories (Pitarque, Vagelnov, Nosko, Hirvonen, Norppa, Crews, et al., 1999). Workers were exposed to acetone, gasoline, and toluene in both factories and to ethylacetate and diisocyanate in one factory. Although exposures did not suggest an association with DNA damage, the exposed workers' blood hemoglobin was lower and their urinary hippuric acid concentration was higher than in the control group (Pitarque et al., 1999). Jöckel, Pohlabeln, Bolm-Audorff, Bruske-Hohlfeld, and Wichmann studied lung cancer risks in German shoe manufacturing and repair workers (Jöckel et al., 2000). They identified all individuals who had ever worked in shoe manufacturing or repair for at least half a year among 4,184 hospital-based lung cancer cases. With smoking and occupational asbestos exposures adjusted, the study demonstrated an increased lung cancer risk among shoe workers which seemed to double after 30 years on the job (Jöckel et al., 2000).

Bulbulyan, Changuina, Zaridze, Astashevsky, Colin, and Boffetta examined whether Moscow shoe factory workers exposed to chloroprene (2-chloro-1,3-butadiene) were at increased risk of cancer (Bulbulyan et al., 1998). Chloroprene is used to manufacture the synthetic rubber polychloroprene used in glues. The chemical structure of chloroprene is similar to that of vinyl chloride, which is strongly associated with liver cancer (angiosarcoma); the study suggested that exposure to chloroprene increases the risk of liver cancer (Bulbulyan et al., 1998). The National Toxicology Program's Report on Carcinogens stated about chloroprene:

> Chloroprene is reasonably anticipated to be a human carcinogen based on evidence of benign and malignant tumors formation at multiple tissue sites in multiple species of experimental animals. (National Toxicology Program, 2002)

Other Health Effects: Reproductive Problems, Liver Damage, and Multiple Solvent Co-Exposure

Some studies also suggest that toluene and aliphatic organic solvents cause reproductive problems—spontaneous abortions, birth defects, and low birth-weight babies (Agnesi, Valentini, & Mastrangelo, 1997; Thomas, 1998). As discussed above, glues are often solvent mixtures (e.g., toluene, acetone, MEK, ethyl acetate, xylene, hexane, and so forth). It is possible that co-exposures could amplify the toxic effects. For example, it has been suggested that MEK may enhance the neurotoxicity of hexane (Nijem, Kristensen, Al-Khatib, Takrori, & Bjertness, 2001). It is important to note that besides solvents, aniline-based dyes can be used in the finishing work. Aniline is known to harm the blood's hemoglobin so that it can not transfer oxygen—this disease is known as methemoglobinemia and its severity depends on the extent of exposure (Agency for Toxic Substances and Disease Registry [ATSDR], 2002).

Tomei, Guintoli, Biagi, Baccolo, Tomao, and Rosati (1999) studied and suggested the possibility of liver damage among shoe repairers. They indicated that exposure even below the threshold limit values may harm various target organs; the specific risk factor was assumed to be an exposure to solvent mixtures (Tomei et al., 1999). Chen and Chan (1999) explained that most of the Taiwanese-manufactured adhesives were either toluene- or MEK-based. Their 1988 study of 468 workers in 17 footwear factories confirmed hazardous effects of toluene-MEK based glues: about half of the female workers and one-third of the male workers had liver-function problems (Chen & Chan, 1999).

To What Extent is Benzene Still Used in Adhesives?

Benzene—a well-documented carcinogen, strongly associated with leukemia and aplastic anemia—was widely used as a glue solvent for shoemaking. In Italy, Vigliani published rising benzene poisoning cases in 1950s— even though there was ample evidence linking job exposure to benzene and cancer, the Italian shoe industry had little incentive to follow up to Vigliani's findings and behaved as if *the death cases were an unavoidable industrial by-product of the economic growth* (Blanc, 2007). By 1970s, pure benzene had finally been removed as an intentional solvent additive from almost all industrial and consumer glues, although it continues to remain as a trace contaminant (Blanc, 2007). For example, toluene often contains traces of benzene: both substances are obtained and produced from the same crude oil distillate fraction, therefore, an industrial grade toluene may contain up to 20% of other hydrocarbons, and especially benzene (Feldman, 1999).

The extent to which benzene-based adhesive may still be used in the world's shoe production is unknown. Chen and Chan pointed out that even though the use of pure benzene-containing adhesives has declined in state-owned enterprises in China during recent decades, poisoning reports in the collective and private factories revealed that workers were still exposed to benzene (Chen & Chan, 1999). The authors interviewed Chinese work safety and health specialists who suggested that benzene-based adhesives seemed to be about 30% cheaper than others. They also discovered a widely held myth among both employers and workers' representatives that benzene-based adhesives have a superior adhesive quality (Chen & Chan, 1999).

Child Shoemakers

The Ulil Albab Health Foundation—a non-government organization (NGO) constituting medical doctors, nurses, and health aides—has been the ILO-IPEC footwear project's key research partner from the very beginning in Bandung, Indonesia. In 2002, the Foundation conducted a study to investigate health problems of 173 child shoemakers. They identified that many of them suffered from headaches, colds, twisted muscles, respiratory diseases like asthma, nose bleeding, hyposmia (the lack of sense of smell), and tuberculosis. The study methods included interviews, physical examinations, and follow-up health monitoring. Thirty-six percent of the children suffered from respiratory problems, 18% from headaches, nearly 10% from digestive system disorders, and several had skin infections, allergies, muscle aches, hypertension, and injuries caused by knives, hammers, and other sharp tools (Hakim, 2003).

The Occupational Safety and Health Center (OSH Center) of the Philippines has done extensive investigations of child footwear workers. In 2001, with the support of ILO-IPEC Footwear project in Biñan, a team of industrial hygienists, occupational health practitioners, and safety engineers from the OSH Center conducted research among child shoemakers in Biñan. The study included health examinations (chest x-ray, blood and urine samples, urine metabolites, questionnaire of specific symptoms) work environment measurements (dust, solvents, illumination, and general ventilation), safety audits of workplaces, and focus group discussions (OSHC, 2001). Forty-seven percent of children began working at age eight or younger. The most important reason that children worked was to help their families to earn income (OSHC, 2001). Health examinations revealed that 33% of children were diagnosed with swollen glands in the neck. Malnutrition was prevalent (OSHC, 2001). Children reported neurological symptoms including forgetfulness, headache, fatigue, and irritability (OSHC, 2001).They felt the most common musculoskeletal pain in their neck, backs (lower and upper backs), shoulders, and knees (OSHC, 2001).

Estrella-Gust, Executive Director of the OSH Center, coordinated another investigation on working conditions of informal sector shoe production in the Philippines. She determined that thousands of children work in the industry (Estrella-Gust, 2000). In addition to a survey, the extensive study included focus groups with industry representatives, site visits, as well as interviews with and physical examinations of child workers. Most worksites were cramped, poorly lit, dusty with poorly ventilated, and in poor sanitary conditions. Solvents exceeded legal exposure limits. This was a concern because living and working quarters were often the same. Yet, employers, parents and children did not consider such risks a major problem (Estrella-Gust, 2000).

SHOEMAKING PROCESS IN HOME-BASED WORKSHOPS

The term "home-based shoe workshop" may seem ambiguous. Here, "home-based shoe workshop" is used interchangeably with home-based shoe manufacturing when any production activity: (a) occurs inside the house, in any part that is connected to the living areas (e.g., kitchen, living-room, garage, storage); or (b) outside, but within the immediate vicinity of the house when the production area is easily accessible to family members. The workshop is not considered home-based if it is not easily accessible to other family members, and if no activities or tasks are done at home.

The size of a home-based establishment varies: the workforce may consist of only the family members—husband, wife, and children—who prepare and stitch uppers, attach the parts together by gluing them in their house. Some home-based shops have a designated area for shoemaking that is separate from the living quarters. In other cases, the workshop may be next to the house. If sales and orders are good, families may recruit outside piece-rate laborers—both skilled shoemakers and workers to carry out other tasks—to help complete the orders.

The number of tasks depends on the kind of shoe being manufactured and the available machinery. In its simplest form, the process flowchart that epitomizes a typical home-based manufacturing enterprise is illustrated in Figure 1.

First, footwear materials (e.g., leather, polyurethane, PVC) for uppers and bottoms are prepared and sorted. Shoe bottoms and uppers are often manufactured elsewhere and arrive ready-made for assembly. Medium and larger shoe enterprises may have a sole molding machine, but this task was not carried out in the home-based shoe workshops I visited in Biñan and Bandung. If uppers are not ready-made, the upper design is drawn on the material according to a pattern, and is then cut with scissors. After cutting, the outer area of the material is thinned with a skiving machine. The uppers and linings are sewn together. Eyeleting, buttonholing, and decorating may be carried out. The uppers and lowers are assembled primarily by gluing, but also by stitching, nailing, or screwing (International Programme on the Elimination of Child Labour [IPEC] & Markkanen, 2002). For all men's and most women's shoes, the last (an artificial foot) is the chief tool used to assist in attaching

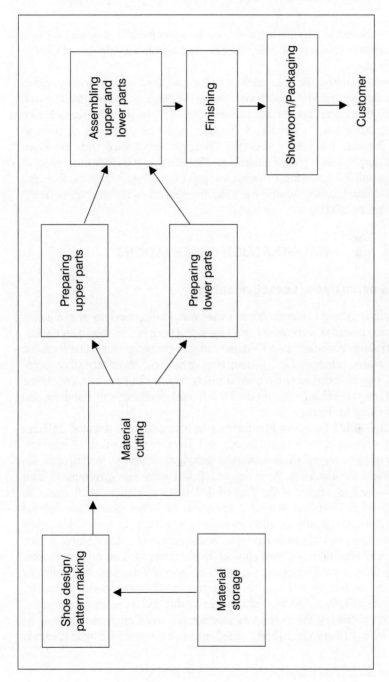

Figure 1. Major operations in home-based footwear outwork manufacturing as observed by the Industrial Design Department of the Bandung University of Technology.

uppers to the insole. The last helps to keep the upper parts in place and to shape them correctly vis-à-vis the sole. Slippers and simple sandals do not usually require a last.

Before assembly, the sole parts may be smoothed with a grinder. Soles that are not ground are treated with primer—often a hazardous MEK-based chemical that cleans the surface and prepares it for more effective adhesive bonding. After glue is spread on the sole, it is heat-treated in an oven to further increase the bond's strength. Then, glue-assembled parts are compressed tightly with a pressing machine. Finishing may include such tasks as cleaning, polishing, waxing, coloring, and paint-spraying. Finally, the footwear is packed into boxes or plastic bags and transported to the customers (IPEC & Markkanen, 2002).

WALK-THROUGH OBSERVATIONS

Assessments by the Local Evaluators

Both in Bandung (Indonesia) and Biñan (the Philippines), local evaluators visited and assessed work safety and health practices in 31[1] shoe manufacturing workshops according to a 16-item worksite evaluation form that included such items as demographics, management practices, chemical safety, ergonomics, psychosocial hazards, overall safety and health practices, etc. These evaluations yielded information on 14 different workshops in Bandung and 17 workshops in Biñan.

The ILO-IPEC Footwear Programmes in both countries selected different types (home-based/ non home-based) and sizes (e.g., number of workers, amount of turnover) of shoe workshops among their project participants. All of the local evaluators in Bandung and Biñan were non-government individuals who had—either at the time of this study or earlier—participated in the ILO-IPEC Footwear project's activities. In Biñan, the author briefed all five assessors jointly on the evaluation form content; nevertheless, they were asked to carry out an independent assessment and not to discuss results, scores, or observations with one another. In Bandung, the four evaluators were the ILO-IPEC's staff members; the IPEC's National Programme Coordinator helped the author by briefing his colleagues one-by-one on the evaluation items, and similarly, asked the evaluators to conduct independent assessments.

In both countries, the evaluators scored each work environment item on a scale from 1 (worst) to 5 (best), noted relevant observations, and whenever

[1] Thirty-one shoe workshops in total, both countries included.

possible, took photos of work practices and working conditions. Besides the scored assessment items, the evaluators collected background information (demographics) on the people who worked in the shoe workshops.

The following section describes both my and the evaluators' observations but does not discuss the scoring details of various work environment assessment items.[2]

What Did We See?

The workshops local evaluators and I visited in Bandung and Biñan shared several dangerous features. The shop space is small, crowded, and without ventilation—it easily starts to resemble a confined space. Some workshops were described as very small, cramped, and with only a little space to move around in. Often, the air hardly circulated inside without fans. Most workshops were too warm and humid during the day. Some places had proper lighting, while others were quite dim. On occasion, windows provided natural light. But, some workshops had one window or no windows at all.

Fire exits seldom exist; there is often only one door to come in and go out. Flammable footwear chemicals are stored in large quantities. Fire extinguishers were rarely available. The potential for fire or explosion hazard is ever-present in neighboring residences and ultimately in the whole village. Knife-sharpening stations, electrical equipment, and burning cigarettes are of common ignition sources. I witnessed a worker use an open gas burner flame to smooth the sides of leather after attaching upper parts to the insole.

Dust and solvent vapors fill the air throughout the work area. Dust is generated from sole grinding and polishing tasks. While grinding was often performed outside the house, the front door area was not necessarily covered and grinding dusts could enter the house. To protect themselves while grinding, some workers covered their noses with their shirts. The solvent exposure is the greatest in adhesive application, stain removal and other cleaning tasks, spray-painting, and polishing. While brushes, toothbrushes, and wooden sticks usually spread the glue, too frequently it was spread with bare fingers. Many of the solvents are also strong irritants. When coupled with the dust, it is not surprising that many workers and their family members—especially small children—develop respiratory problems. Coughs, bronchitis, and asthma are frequent health disorders. In one family in Biñan, all four children had asthma.

---

[2]Scoring details and the 16-item worksite evaluation form is presented in the author's doctoral dissertation.

The evaluators paid special attention to chemical storage practices and whether work areas were located dangerously near or safely away from cooking appliances. In both countries, the chemicals were inadequately labeled or not labeled at all. Information on ingredients used, hazards, and handling precautions were seldom provided. Operators and workers were somewhat alert to the effects of chemicals on their health. A few Biñan business owners labeled the chemicals themselves and stored them in one place.

Air quality is a problem because exhaust ventilation is not structurally or economically feasible in most smaller workshops and houses. The equipment also is expensive—both to purchase and maintain. In the Philippines, table fans were used in many workshops and doors kept open to allow natural ventilation. While standing or ceiling fans are better than nothing, they are not an ideal prevention method and precautions in their use are seldom taken. They can provide relief in some circumstances, for example, to reduce heat. However, they do not eliminate solvents and dusts from the house but may circulate them more widely inside the house. In addition, fan motors can set off sparks and be a fire hazard.

Separating the work area from the living area and applying glues outdoors or in the least confined atmospheres were one of the most effective preventive interventions against solvent exposures I observed. These measures tended to be coupled with improved housekeeping practices which varied from one workplace to another; some owners made serious efforts but more often than not housekeeping tended to be neglected: shoe materials, chemical containers, and tools were scattered around. Some workshops had proper waste containers outside the house or workers used sacks to gather material remnants.

The workers I observed smoked cigarettes almost everywhere, even over an open glue bowl. Only a few workshops prohibited smoking. Quite often, food often was consumed in the production areas. Food was sometimes provided by managers but this meant that work continued while workers ate. There appeared to be a good relationship among workers and managers. Workers appeared to have a chance to communicate and interact with co-workers. Although some managers taught workers proper work practices and supervised them closely, there was little if any instruction on hazards and how to work safely. Mostly, workshop owners had learned about work dangers from their parents. In Biñan, the local evaluators reported that children were not directly involved in hazardous manufacturing phases, however, they were observed making shoeboxes.

A common work posture is to sit cross-legged or squat on the floor. Workers also may sit on a bench or stool. When chairs with backrests are provided, they often are plastic garden-type chairs. These chairs are not very comfortable to sit in for several hours, and not surprisingly, workers may find sitting on

Figure 2. Glue application and polishing tasks in the footwear
workshops of Biñan (top) and Bandung (bottom).
Photographs taken by the author.

the floor cross-legged more natural and comfortable. Glue containers became improvised chairs. If workstations existed, they generally were not designed for the worker's anthropometrics: too small workplaces do not provide enough space for decent workstations. Spacious workshops had such items as chairs with backrests and tables. In bigger workshops, there were plenty of storage areas and ample space to move around.

No heavy loads were handled. Task repetitiveness varied. Skilled shoemakers had many more task variations than piece-rate workers who were primarily responsible for stitching uppers, cutting material patterns, or gluing parts. Ergonomic hazards originated from awkward postures, repetitive tasks, various tools and equipment that are neither (i) well maintained, and therefore, more force is required when using them, (ii) nor properly designed for the users, therefore not comfortable to handle (e.g., pliers, scissors). For example, adhesive tape was wrapped around bare metal scissor handles to make them more ergonomic.

In small work areas, accident hazards included falls, slips, trips, punctures from protruding wall nails and hooks, cuts, and electrocutions from low hanging electrical wires. Owners and staff did not recall any serious accidents. They told evaluators only about cuts, punctures, and hits from sharp tools or hammers. Sometimes, shoes were hammered on the lap. The common tools and equipment used were lasts, scissors, knives, skivers, cutting machines, hammers, sewing machines, ovens, and pressing machines. Evaluators marked the lack of protective machine guards. In one 35-person workplace in Biñan, sewing and grinding machines were described to generate noise.

Most places, even the small ones, had a toilet, sink, and water. One space might serve as a combined dining, sleeping, and working area. Mostly, a separate rest area existed for workers. The condition of buildings varied and different houses might be attached to one another. Sometimes, ceilings were low. Walls could be made of wood or concrete and roofs were described as made of galvanized iron sheets.

INDONESIAN SHOE PRODUCERS: INTERVIEW FINDINGS

Home-based shoemaking is piece-rate work with no fixed working hours (see Figure 3). Generally, work started at 8-9 A.M. and lasted 10 or more hours. Working until 10 P.M. was common when orders needed to be filled. A shoemaker couple might work from 7:00 A.M. until noon, take a short break, and continue working until 4 P.M. But when there were lots of orders, they worked into the late evening. When *tukangs* needed money, they worked 15 hours, slept a bit, and started in again.

Figure 3. A boy prepares shoe upper parts in Bandung, Indonesia.
Source: InFocus Programme for the Elimination of Child Labour (IPEC)
of the International Labour Organization (ILO), (Ruhiat, 2002).

The interviews confirmed my and local evaluators' observations. Shoe workshops are filled with hazardous exposures to glues, primers, and cleaning agents, unguarded tools, and dust. Work positions are often awkward, cuts and burns are common, as are respiratory disorders. Asthma and breathing difficulties were widespread when primers were in use. Workers were reluctant to visit doctors because of the expense.

Mr. Salet—a well-known shoe brand manufacturer—burns shoe threads to clean them and removes glue stains with gasoline. Once, he produced everything at home but realized that it was unsafe for his daughters to with sharp tools and solvent vapors. He moved his *bengkel* outside, but next to his house. Ms. Dessy—the business manager—renovated her *bengkel* right before the interview and mentioned that glues were no longer stored next to stoves.

There were mixed feelings in the community regarding work health and safety. Mr. and Mrs. Dahn alleged, that many Cibaduyut residents took shoemaking more seriously than their health. Consequently, they were skeptical toward health promotion. With shoes the source of their bread, *"don't-exploit-children"* and *"glues-are-dangerous"* represented idealistic rhetoric which menaced their livelihood. Mr Dahn said:

> If they (tukangs) want to drink coffee (in the bengkel) and need something to stir it, they just take any object nearby to stir it. They think "gurih katanya haha" people here get immune. And outsiders who have never smelled glue are more susceptible and get sick. (Mr. Dahn, homeworker, interviewed in Bandung)

The *Tukang's* administrator—Mr. Annan— stated that after several ILO-IPEC's discussions, many people realized that it was bad to store glues at home. While he noted that it would be better to separate the working and living spaces he doubted that most people would do so. Workplace safety and health awareness will take time. People thought that the OSH training and information from the Ulil Albab Foundation and the ILO-IPEC were all very good, however they doubted its applicability in the field. After the training, some people were scared about hazards but many continued their production practices as before.

Mr. Iman, business owner, improved lighting and ventilation in his *bengkel*. He also provided simple dust masks for his laborers and gave workers a toothbrush for applying glue. Ms. Dessy provided gloves for *tukang*s but noted that her workers did not use them all the time. She made the glove use optional. Mr. Ari, skilled shoemaker, believed that safety and health promotion made sense because most *bengkel*s in Cibaduyut continued to operate as they had been doing for years. He indicated that owners rarely thought about air circulation or knew very much about work safety.

Mr. Eni did not want his children in the shoe industry. For him, the work was dangerous, so he hoped they would find better jobs. Mr. Saleh stated that safety and health was each owner's individual responsibility. He wanted his workers to exercise every Monday—he gave them snacks and money to play soccer. People thought that he was very generous. At the same time, he motivated his workers to keep working and stay healthy. It was also an incentive to get them to work on Monday morning. Some people in Cibaduyut only reluctantly worked on Mondays if they had money left from the weekend. Every Saturday, his workers played badminton together.

PHILIPPINE SHOE PRODUCERS:
INTERVIEW FINDINGS

When there are large orders, workers toil around the clock. Mrs. Francis worked on shoe patterns from 8 A.M. until 5 P.M. When there was a rush job, work lasted until midnight. Mrs. Martinez explained that there were no set hours. She started at 8 A.M. and continued until 9 P.M., while her husband might work until 1 or 2 A.M., sleeping just two hours a day during the peak production season. They did not hire outside laborers. Mrs. John said that she and her husband started work at 8 A.M. after sending the children to school, took a break at 11 A.M. and resumed work at 1 P.M., continuing until 7 or 8 P.M.

Mrs. Eno, a subcontractor, stayed in Biñan on Mondays and Thursdays to oversee her shoe producers. On Tuesdays, Wednesdays, Fridays, and Saturdays, she went to their wholesale store to meet customers. On store days, Mrs. Eno usually left at 3 A.M., stayed until noon, and returned to Biñan. Ms. Lane, another subcontractor, mentioned that, in principle, she could start whenever she wished but her usual schedule was from 7 A.M. to 7 P.M. Their piece-rate workers could start or rest at any time. They might work from 7 A.M. to 8 P.M., or even to 10 P.M. Sometimes, workers took lunch at noon, and rested until 3 P.M.

Shoe producers in Biñan participated in work safety and health training courses[3] and internalized basic injury and health hazard prevention practices. They learned that footwear chemicals were hazardous, and as a result, many of them set up a divider to separate the living and work areas and keep chemicals stored away from cooking appliances. But, some tasks like shoe cleaning that workers did not consider hazardous were carried out in the living room.

When work-related accidents and adverse health effects were out of sight, they remained out of mind with few precautions taken. People believed that glues, primers, and paints did not affect their health. When learning the trade, apprentices often hit themselves with hammers or pricked themselves with needles. Serious injuries included cuts and wounds with scissors, sharp cutting tools, and finishing blades. Workers suffered from chest pains, breathing difficulties, and backaches and allergies, asthma, and tuberculosis were not uncommon.

One shoemaker stated that workers and business owners did not heed safety. "*Workers simply work and work.*" Glues sometimes were applied with bare hands. Mrs. Lane found it dangerous to inhale adhesives, but for her, there was nothing to do about it. Shoemakers bore the responsibility. The representative of the local footwear association, remarked:

[3] Organized by the OSH Center and ILO-IPEC Footwear Team in Biñan.

... it is not so safe to have this kind of industry in their area. The people are not aware of the hazards of the chemicals being used.

Work safety and health is not considered a priority because the government does not expect very much from small firms. The representative continued:

> And I believe that if I ask the help of the local legislators in the Municipality to have OSH program, they will definitely help me, and the association. Before, nobody was speaking for the sector. While formal organizations of small manufacturers existed before, these organizations were only concerned about soliciting funds from the government. They were not really organized to look after the welfare of the manufacturers and workers. So, I hope under my leadership, the manufacturers, workers and local government units will become more concerned about OSH. (The representative of the local footwear association, interviewed in Biñan)

The Biñan community organizer, Mr. Smith, noted that larger operators can separate work and living areas. Because a typical house in Biñan is very small, about 20 square meters, work and living spaces become harder to separate. There is usually a small window for air circulation. The sleeping quarters, working area, and kitchen are often one room. When laborers applied adhesives, in such small spaces, the fumes made them drunk. Children's safety and health was affected:

> People are hard-headed. They would say: "This is our work. And in this work, we earn money. If you give us money so that we will not do this footwear work, it's okay. But if you do not give us money, we cannot make any solution because this footwear work is what makes our family survive." So that's my challenge. I want them to be aware of safety and health. But mostly ... 90 percent of the small footwear operators would answer back every time I would say to them to keep their tools away from their children that: "We have no other place, only this, because we are only squatting on this area." (Mr. Smith, community organizer, interviewed in Biñan)

CONCLUSION

The workplace evaluations by local assessors and my own walk-through observations revealed a number of hazards in shoe workshops. The combined exposures to dust and solvents are associated with various health effects and safety concerns. Shoe manufacturing will remain a hazardous occupation as long as organic solvents are applied in the production. It is notable that in 1912, the Massachusetts[4] Health Inspection report declared that naphtha cement, then in use for footwear manufacturing, was considered hazardous work. The 1912

---

[4]Major footwear manufacturing Center in the United States during 1800-1950.

report also referred to a law which required the exclusion of minors from occupations hazardous to health—the naphtha cement use was considered such hazardous work unless a mechanical means of ventilation was provided and the cement containers were covered (State Board of Health, 1912). Minors were prohibited from using the cement. Almost a century later, hazardous footwear chemicals are still applied—even by children—in the global footwear industry.

REFERENCES

Agency for Toxic Substances and Disease Registry (ASTDR). (2002). *Aniline fact sheet.* ASTDR, Division of Toxicology. Retrieved at: http://www.atsdr.cdc.gov/tfacts171.pdf

Agnesi, R., Valentini, F., & Mastrangelo, G. (1997). Risk of spontaneous abortion and maternal exposure to organic solvents in the shoe industry. *International Archives of Environmental Health, 69,* 311-316.

Blanc, P. D. (2007). *How everyday products make people sick: Toxins at home and in the workplace.* Berkeley, CA: University of California Press.

Bovenzi, M., Fiorito, A., & Patussi, V. (1990). Esthesiometric thresholds in workers exposed to neuropathogenic chemical and physical agents (in Italian). *La Medicina del Lavoro, 81*(1), 22-31.

Bulbulyan, M. A., Changuina, O. V., Zaridze, D. G., Astashevsky, S. V., Colin, D., & Boffetta, P. (1998). Cancer mortality among Moscow shoe workers exposed to chloroprene. *Cancer Causes and Control, 9,* 381-387.

Cardona, A., Marhuenda, D., Marti, J., Brugnone, F., Roel, J., & Perbellini, L. (1993). Biological monitoring of occupational exposure to n-hexane by measurement of urinary 2,5-hexanedione. *International Archives of Occupational and Environmental Health, 65*(1), 71-74.

Chen, M., & Chan, A. (1999). China's "market economics in command": Footwear workers' health in jeopardy. *International Journal of Health Services, 29*(4), 793-811.

Conradi, F. L., & Portich, P. (1998). Footwear Industry. In J. Stellman (Ed.), *The ILO encyclopaedia on occupational health and safety* (4th ed., Vol. 3, pp. 88.1-88.12). Geneva: International Labour Office (ILO).

Constatini, A. S, Quinn, M., Consonni, D., & Zappa, M. (2003). Exposure to benzene and risk of leukemia among shoe factory workers. *Scandinavian Journal of Work Environment and Health, 29*(1), 51-59.

Decoufle, P., & Walrath, J. (1987). Nasal cancer in the US shoe industry: Does it exist? *American Journal of Industrial Medicine, 12,* 605-613.

Estrella-Gust, D. P. (2000). A case study on child labour in the Philippine footwear industry: Health, safety and work Environment. *Asian Pacific Newsletter on Occupational Health and Safety, 7*(2), 41-45.

Feldman, R. G. (1999). *Occupational and environmental neurotoxicology* (pp. 253-254). Philadelphia, PA: Lippincott–Raven Publishers.

Fu, H., Demers, P. A., Costantini, A. S., Winter, P., Colin, D., Kogevinas, M., & Boffetta, P. (1996). Cancer mortality among shoe manufacturing workers: An analysis of two cohorts. *Occupational and Environmental Medicine, 53*(6), 394-398.

Garabrant, D. H., & Wegman, D. H. (1984). Cancer mortality among shoe and leather workers in Massachusetts. *American Journal of Industrial Medicine, 5,* 303-314.

Hakim, A. (2003). *The improvement of safety and health of workers as an avenue into eliminating child labour in the informal footwear sector: The ILO/IPEC Footwear Team's and its Partners' experience in Cibaduyut, Bandung, Indonesia.* Paper presented at the National Occupational Safety and Health Conference, in Jakarta, January 13, 2003.

InFocus Programme for the Elimination of Child Labour (IPEC) Footwear Team in Bandung, & Markkanen, P. (2003). *Improving safety, health and the working environment in the informal footwear sector.* Jakarta: International Labour Office (ILO).

International Agency for Research of Cancer (IARC). (1981). *Monographs on the evaluation of the carcinogenic risk of chemicals to humans: Wood, leather and some associated industries* (Vol. 25). Lyon: IARC.

International Agency for Research on Cancer (IARC). (1999). Dichloromethene. *IARC Summaries and Evaluations, 71,* 251. Retrieved at: http://www.inchem.org

International Textile, Garment and Leather Workers' Federation (ITGLF). (2002). ITGLF press release, May 29, 2002. Blaze in Indian shoe factory kills 44: Global union demands measures to clean up industry. Retrieved at: http://www.itglwf.org/

Jöckel, K. H., Pohlabeln, H., Bolm-Audorff, U., Bruske-Hohlfeld, I., & Wichmann, H. E. (2000). Lung cancer risk of workers in shoe manufacture and repair. *American Journal of Industrial Medicine, 37*(6), 575-580.

Lee, D. H., Park, I. G., Kim, J. H., Lee, T. H., Kim, D., & Kang, S. (1998). Neurobehavioural changes in shoe manufacturing workers. *Neurotoxicology and Teratogenicity, 20*(3), 259-263.

Mayan, O., Pires, A., Neves, P., & Capela, F. (1999). Shoe manufacturing and solvent exposure in northern Portugal. *Applied Occupational and Environmental Hygiene, 14*(11), 785-790.

National Toxicology Program. (2002, December). Report on carcinogens 10th ed.). U.S. Department of Health and Human Services, Public Health Service. Retrieved at: http://ehp.niehs.nih.gov/roc/toc10.html

Nijem, K., Kristensen, P., Al-Khatib, A., Takrori, F., & Bjertness, E. (2001). Prevalence of neuropsychiatric and mucous membrane irritation complaints among Palestinian shoe factory workers exposed to organic solvents and plastic compounds. *American Journal of Industrial Medicine, 40*(2), 192-198.

Nijem, K., Kristensen, P., Thorud, S. Al-Khatib, A., Takrori, F., & Bjertness, E. (2001). Solvent exposures at shoe factories and workshops in Hebron City, West Bank. *International Journal of Occupational and Environmental Health, 7,* 182-188.

Occupational Safety and Health Center (OSHC). (2001). The blight in the footwear industry: Assessment of the safety, health and environment of child workers/ laborers in the footwear industry in Biñan, Laguna, and the Philippines. The Department of Labor and Employment (DOLE), the Philippines.

Passero, S., Battistini, N., Cioni, R., Giannini, F., Paradiso, C., Battista, et al. (1983). Toxic polyneuropathy of shoe workers in Italy: A clinical, neurophysiological and follow-up study. *Italian Journal of Neurological Science, 4*(4), 463-472.

Pitarque, M., Vaglenov, A., Nosko, M., Hirvonen, A., Norppa, H., Creus, A., & Marcos, R. (1999). Evaluation of DNA damage by the comet assay in shoe workers exposed to toluene and other organic solvents. *Mutation Research, 441*(1), 115-127.

State Board of Health. (1912). *Hygiene of the boot and shoe industry in Massachusetts.* Boston, MA: Wright & Potter Printing Co.

Thomas, K. (1998). Solvents used in the production of footwear. *Maquila Solidarity Network.* Retrieved at:
http://www.maquilasolidarity.org/campaigns/nike/solvents.htm

Tomei, F., Guintoli, P., Biagi, M., Baccolo, T. P., Tomao, E., & Rosati, M. V. (1999). Liver damage among shoe repairers. *American Journal of Industrial Medicine, 36,* 541-547.

Valentini, F., Agnesi, R., Dal Vecchio, L., Fabbro, A., Gasparini, N., Gori, G., et al. (1994). Exposure to glues containing technical heptane: A clinical and electro-physiological study (in Italian). *La Medicina del Lavoro, 85*(6), 514-521.

Walrath, J., Decoufle, P., & Thomas, T. L. (1987). Mortality among workers in a shoe manufacturing company. *American Journal of Industrial Medicine, 12,* 615-623.

Ward, E. M., Burnett, C. A., Ruder, A., & Davis-King, K. (1997). Industries and cancer. *Cancer Causes and Control, 8,* 356-370.

Watfa, N., Awan, S., & Goodson, R. (1998). Chemical risk assessment and occupational hygiene preventive measures in small and medium-sized enterprises. Geneva: International Labour Office (ILO). Retrieved at:
http://www.ilo.org/public/english/protection/safework/papers/smechem/index.htm

Zuskin, E., Mustajbegovic, J., Schachter, E. N., Doko-Jelinic, J., & Bradic, V. (1997). Respiratory function in shoe manufacturing workers. *American Journal of Industrial Medicine, 31*(1), 50-55.

CHAPTER 3

Informal Sector, Informal Economy

Does home-based shoemaking represent a typical informal sector workplace? The bigger picture of the informal sector deserves its own discussion to enable us to seek underlying forces that engender hazardous conditions where occupational and public health concerns converge. Furthermore, this sector comprises the majority of the global labor force.

The term *informal sector* was first used in the International Labour Organization's (ILO)'s pioneering 1972 report on Kenya: it referred to workers who were not recognized, recorded, protected, and regulated by public authorities (Tokman, 2001). Twenty years later, the 1991 ILO Director General's Report noted:

> There can be no question of the ILO helping to promote or develop an informal sector as a convenient, low-cost way of creating employment unless there is at the same time an equal determination to eliminate progressively the worst aspects of exploitation and inhuman working conditions in the sector. (ILO, 1991)

Tokman pinpointed three distinctive informal sector attributes evolving from the pioneering Kenya report and from more recent studies and surveys: (a) Working poor. The problem of employment in developing countries is not unemployment, but workers who do not earn enough to make a living, including: feeding the family, gaining access to decent healthcare and education, or being able to afford safe housing. (b) Survival. People seek low-productivity income-earning alternatives that may provide for their survival. (c) Global-ization and international division of labor. To deal with unstable demands, enterprises introduce more flexible and decentralized production systems to cut the costs and externalize demand fluctuations (Tokman, 2001).

Even today, the vast majority of the people in the informal sector work hard to survive, often without decency and dignity. The 2002 ILO's Conference report points out that different groups—workers and entrepreneurs—have been termed "informal" because of one chief characteristic: they are not recognized or protected under the legal and regulatory frameworks (ILO, 2002a). People are highly vulnerable: when little or no legal or social protection is granted, they cannot enforce contracts or own property. While they work, there is little safety, benefits are lacking, working time is long, and skills development possibilities are scarce. They are also highly dependent on public authorities who often confuse them with criminals and subject them to harassment and extortion (ILO, 2002).

Hernando De Soto described Peruvian workers in the informal sector as "extralegal" entrepreneurs who together with their extended families con-stitute about 60–80% of the country's population (De Soto, 1989). In 1986, the Institute for Liberty and Democracy (ILC)—spearheaded by De Soto—established the nation's first "*ombudsman*" for all citizens; in 1993, this position was institutionalized by the new Constitution, and at that time, a call for grievances was put forward (De Soto, 1989). During the first month, the ILC received complaints from 153 civic organizations representing about 300,000 individuals: the primary concerns were about difficulties gaining legal access to property—houses, offices, factories, or agricultural land—and obstacles when trying to initiate and run their businesses. He stated that *property is more than ownership—it is the hidden architecture that organizes the market economy in Western countries*. International globalization per se is not the only reason why capitalism fails in developing countries but because developing countries have been *unable to "globalize" capital within their own countries* (De Soto, 2000).

The global NGO called Women in Informal Employment Globalizing and Organizing (WIEGO) prefers using the term "informal economy" for "informal sector," albeit precariousness remains the chief defining character in both terms (WIEGO, 2003). The term "economy" makes clear that informality is not confined to a certain sector of economic activity and emphasizes the connectedness between the informal and formal activities (WIEGO, 2003). WIEGO researchers have analyzed and provided the ILO with a statistical assessment of the size of the informal economy. A broadly defined informal employment comprises 47–72% of non-agricultural workforce in developing countries, as follows: 47% in the Middle East and North Africa; 51% in Latin

America; 71% in Asia; and 72% in sub-Saharan Africa (ILO, 2002b). When agricultural activities were included in the estimates, the informal employment estimates are much higher, for example: 83–93% in India, 55–62% in Mexico, and 28–34% in South Africa (ILO, 2002b).

The vast majority of informal sector workforce are women. Home-based workers and street vendors are the two largest informal employment sector groups representing 10 to 25% of the non-agricultural workforce in developing countries—80% or more of industrial outworkers who work at home are female (ILO, 2002b). Chen suggests that a major reason for this is because all of the world's cultures perceive that women are responsible for childcare and household work, not because women have fewer skills than men to compete in the labor market outside home (Chen, 1991). Tomei, in her ILO report on homeworkers in Latin America, contended that subcontracting has contributed to a redefinition of the relationship between the formal and informal economies (Tomei, 2000). These economies were conceived as two separate entities that coexisted within a single economic context. However, the formal and informal sectors form increasingly close links through the globalization process (Tomei, 2000).

WHAT IS HOME WORK?

"Home work" is still a debated term. Is a homeworker really a worker or self-employed? The ILO's Home Work Convention, adopted in 1996, provides more clarity and defines home work as follows:

> The term home work is carried out by a person, to be referred to as a homeworker (I) in his or her home or in other premises of his or her choice, other than the workplace of the employer, (ii) for remuneration; (iii) which results in a product or service as specified by the employer, irrespective of who provides the equipment, materials or other inputs used, unless this person has the degree of autonomy and of economic independence necessary to be considered an independent worker under national laws, regulations, or court decisions. (ILO, 1996)

By 2007, five countries had ratified the convention: Albania (2002), Argentina (2006), Finland (1998), Ireland (1999), the Netherlands (2002). The Convention (No. 177, 1996) excludes workers who do not have a subordinate relationship with employers and who establish their own direct relationship with the consumer of the end-product (ILO, 1996). Dependence on an employer, an absence of control over production methods, and work for wages are precise differences between homeworkers and the self-employed, who often use their homes as a workplace (ILO, 1996). Though a lot of necessary work takes place at home, household work and childcare, and "bringing work home from the office" do not constitute homework (Hennon, Locker, & Walker, 2000). Prügl and Tinker describe four home work categories. The first is **industrial home work or outwork**: it is common in the labor-intensive phases of like footwear, electronics, garment production, cigarette rolling, and other (Prügl & Tinker, 1997). **Crafts production** includes basket-weaving, pottery makers, and ornaments makers (Prügl & Tinker, 1997). The third category is people who **make and sell food on the street** or in small stores (Prügl & Tinker, 1997). The fourth category represents **new forms of home-based work** (white-collar homeworkers), including data-entry clerks, translators, computer programmers, typists, and telemarketers (Prügl & Tinker, 1997).

Mass production has not expanded significantly in most developing countries while home-based work has (Chen, Jhabvala, & Lund, 2002). Such outsourcing minimizes labor costs and reduces major investments in land, rent, building, and technology. It allows companies the flexibility to adapt to market fluctuations (Chen et al., 2002; Heikel, 2000; Tokman, 2000). Outworkers do not have guaranteed contracts (Chen et al., 2002). During periods of slow production, homeworkers may work for several employers, making it difficult to establish the social responsibility inherent in the employment relationship (Heikel, 2000). Heikel notes that placing work off the company's premises disguises the employment relationship and usually relieves the employer of social responsibilities: reduction of on-site plant and machinery costs may help medium-sized enterprises appear like small ones; this may entitle them to particular credits and tax advantages (Heikel, 2000). According to Carnoy, economic competition and globalization have created decentralized management. This favors work segregation, task division, and subcontracting a temporary workforce. While the "core work" of production is multi-tasked and carried out by teams, the "non-core" work is carried out by women (Carnoy, 1999).

WOMEN—
THE DESIRED INDUSTRIAL OUTWORKERS

Much of literature on home work indicates that women workers are considered desirable because they are docile, quiet, conscientious, hard-working, and when financially constrained, easy to subdue. Susilastuti profiled Javanese perspectives on the home-based garment industry work. Workers complained that the peak season seemed to become shorter and the lean season longer (Susilastuti, 1996). Workers were required to equip themselves with machines, materials, and transportation equipment. Many women belittled their own economic contribution to the household, for example:

> It is true that both I and my husband work. But he is the breadwinner. His main activity is sewing. I, on the other hand do not only sew. I have to cook, take care of children, and do other chores. As a result, my husband does more work than I do. (Susilastuti, 1996)

In rural areas of Asia and Latin America, women adopted home work as a new income-earning strategy. They were frequently characterized as idle housewives whose work was just a hobby:

> Jobs are sex typed and home work is no exception. The fact that home work is so heavily feminized reflects social constructions of home work as women's work. (Prügl, 1999)

Quite often, homeworkers were not paid a minimum wage even in industrialized countries. In-depth interviews with Chinese-speaking homeworkers in the Ontario area where the minimum wage at that time was $6 CDN an hour, revealed most of them earned on average $4.64 CDN an hour (Dagg, 1996). Their status as immigrants and mothers often left women with little option but to turn to home work. Most women turned to home work because they could not afford child care. More than two-thirds said they would rather work outside the home (Dagg, 1996). As a result of their isolation, many homeworkers suffered from depression, stress, and feelings of powerlessness in the face of low pay and poor work conditions (Tate, 1996).

Garment homeworkers in Bulacan, the Philippines, who preferred home work did so for the following reasons: flexibility to tend both household and income-generating activities and personal control over work hours. Those who preferred factory work did so for higher wages, steady or regular income, concentration on the job, the security and benefits that came with being able to unionize, and the possibility to force their husbands and children to share housework (Pidena-Ofreneo, 1993). Factory work seemed to give women better opportunities to increase their knowledge, consciousness, and experience (Pidena-Ofreneo, 1993).

REFLECTIONS FROM INDONESIA

Indonesian Work Safety and Health Infrastructure

The most significant Indonesian occupational safety and health (OSH) law is the *Work Safety Act* (No. 1, 1970). It stipulates that the Department of

Manpower and Transmigration (DEPNAKER[1]) is responsible for setting up national OSH policy to ensure universal implementation of the law. *The Health Law* (No. 23, 1992) falls under the jurisdiction of the Department of Health. Article 23 on occupational health states that all workers should work at optimal productivity without endangering themselves or their community. It also contains a labor protection program (Occupational Health Centre, 2002). Specific regulations for the mining, nuclear power, and oil and gas industry fall under the jurisdiction of several agencies including the Department of Health, the Department of Mining and Energy, and the Department of Industry (Topobroto, 2002).

In 2001, Indonesia, like many other countries, confronts OSH infrastructure limitations: a shortage of inspectors, constrained resources to conduct an adequate number of thorough inspections, lack of follow-ups after violations, and rarely issued citations. Indonesia's labor force was estimated at 95.7 million, 58.8 million men and 36.9 million women (Department of Health, 2002). Over 45% work in agriculture. More than 60% of the labor force were in the informal sector (ADB, 2002; Department of Health, 2002). After 1984, safety inspections were decentralized with authority transferred to provincial governments. Approximately 1,400 inspectors at the Directorate General of Labour Inspection of DEPNAKER conduct worksite inspections nationwide (Topobroto, 2002). About 400 inspectors are qualified for OSH inspection (Topobroto, 2002).

According to Jacob Nuwa Wea, the Minister of Manpower and Transmigration, work accidents resulted in the loss of 71 million work hours and 340 billion rupiahs in profit (*The Jakarta Post*, 2002). Recorded workplace injuries climbed from 98,902 in 2000 to 104,774 in 2001. During the first half of 2002 alone, there were 57,972 recorded work accidents (Taufiqurrahman & Unidjaja, 2003). The 2003 National OSH Campaign was extensively reported on by the national newspapers. The chairperson of the National Tripartite Occupational Safety and Health Council (DK3N[2]) reported that at the end of 2002, out of the 170,000 companies operating in Indonesia, only 80 had been granted zero accident certification. The director of the Center for Development of Occupational Safety and Health (HIPERKES[3]) stated that the Work Safety Law was too lenient (Taufiqurrahman, 2003). Even President Megawati Soekarnoputri urged companies to improve workplace safety in response to reports about increased fatalities in the workplace

[1]DEPNAKER stands for Departemen Tenaga Kerja dan Transmigrasi.
[2]DK3N stands for Dewan Keselamatan dan Kesehatan Kerja Nasional.
[3]HIPERKES stands for Pusat Bengembaugan Keselamatan Kerja dan Hiperkes.

(Taufiqurrahman, 2003). The Minister of Manpower and Transmigration asserted that DEPNAKER would not hesitate to take stern action against companies violating standard safety measures. He pointed out that a lack of discipline among workers and owners contributed to the increasing number of work-related accidents and illnesses (Taufiqurrahman & Unidjaja, 2003). He added:

> The government lacks the personnel to oversee the law's implementation, and to complicate matters, some of the officials practice corruption, collusion and nepotism with the business owners. (Taufiqurrahman & Unidjaja, 2003)

Indonesia is one of the Asian countries with a regulation mandating an OSH management system (OSH-MS) at large (more than 100 employees) or high-risk enterprises (Department of Manpower and Transmigration [DEPNAKER], 1996). Some perceive an OSH-MS as effective in dealing with challenges in the globalization era. It is not easy to persuade companies to implement OSH-MS or any other OSH policies. In Indonesia, out of 170,000 enterprises that required an OSH-MS by January 2003, only about 500 of them were audited for it (Taufiqurrahman & Unidjaja, 2003). When medium, small, and micro enterprises are taken into account, the number of establishments is in the millions (Rudjito, 2002).[4] The Manpower Act of 2003 strengthened the requirement for OSH-MS. The Act's Article 87 states:

> Every enterprise is under an obligation to apply an occupational safety and health management system that shall be integrated into the enterprise's management system. (State Gazette of the Republic of Indonesia, 2003)

Occupational health services are the mandate of the Occupational Health Centre, under the Secretariat General of the Department of Health. The Centre is divided into (a) an Occupational Health Services Section, (b) an Occupational and Environmental Health Section, and (c) an Administrative Unit (Occupational Health Centre, 2002). The Centre has set up a Strategic Plan in occupational health to carry out its nationwide efforts.

---

[4]The World Bank classification defines: (a) micro enterprises as individuals/firms with total assets less than $100,000, total sales less than $100,000 and employing fewer than 10 persons; (b) small enterprises have total assets or annual sales of $100,000–$3 million and employ 11–50 persons; (c) medium enterprises have total assets or annual sales of more than $3 million and up to $15 million and employ 51–300 persons (Rudjito, 2002).

Informal Sector Work Environment

Although some success stories have emerged on organizing informal sector workers, the vast majority remain unorganized and most trade unions do not try to organize them. An employers' representative from Indonesia I interviewed noted that the informal sector work environment needs governmental interagency attention. In addition to workplace safety and health education, workers needed help on how to run their businesses. He said:

> Firstly, how to improve the management, how to not only survive and develop, and therefore the Department of Industry and Trade is the most important source. The informal sector workers need more funds, small credits, and advice how to manage these funds. Secondly, how could they promote their sells (sales) and products? And how to address the OSH in the workplace: improve ventilation, not using certain hazardous solvent-based glues but water-based ones, improve ergonomics, and all in all, how to be in line with the regulations. (Employers representative, interviewed in Jakarta)

The Department of Health has been involved in informal sector work for several years. A high-level officer explained that the Department is developing a micro health insurance program for informal sector workers.

> . . . for the informal sector, you don't have (necessarily) the employer. You have to be relying upon this worker on capacity to pay; then of course we cannot aim at the highest level of benefit package. We try to give them only a basic benefit package according to their ability to pay. We have developed what we call community (-based) health funding among the working population. (Government representative at the Department of Health, interviewed in Jakarta)

The Indonesian Department of Health services are delivered in 4,300 places to informal sector workers across the country (UKK[5] posts) (Ahmadi & Wibisana, 1997; Joedoatmodjo, 1999) by more than 3,000 public health officers (Topobroto, 2002). Besides increasing availability of occupational health services, the Department of Health aims to implement occupational health programs in the community, foster collaboration between health agencies and workers, and enhance inter-governmental coordination (Ahmadi & Wibisana, 1997; Joedoatmodjo, 1999). The Department of Health instituted several pilot projects to implement primary health care-based occupational health services as close as possible to where people lived and worked. They

[5]UKK stands for Upaya Kesehatan Kerja and translates into Occupational Health Efforts.

provide basic first-aid services after accidents, treat general diseases among workers, encourage the utilization of safety equipment, and organize environmental health programs (Ahmadi & Wibisana, 1997; Joedoatmodjo, 1999).

Rural and urban informal sector workers—mostly women and children—suffer from low nutrition and parasitic diseases. Specific diagnoses by medical doctors include: high lead levels in blood among battery workers, decreased lung function among wood cottage workers, dermatitis among soybean workers, pterigium among fishermen, and eardrum damage among pearl divers (Ahmadi & Wibisana, 1997). Sulistomo describes diseases that are common among women in the informal economy including malnutrition, anemia, infectious diseases, high blood pressure, malaria, visual problems, hearing loss, pesticide poisonings, and respiratory ailments. With little knowledge of health risks at work, economic pressures force women to work long hours with little rest and recovery time (Sulistomo, 1997). Sulistomo reported on three case studies. The first was a 60-year-old woman, widowed for 26 years, with two children. She washed clothes and suffered from a tumor near her right eye which was diagnosed as a type of skin cancer. The second was a 36-year-old married woman with two children who had worked for 10 years as a seamstress in a home-based workshop. She complained of weakness in her left hand and a physical examination indicated that she was underweight, anemic, and suffered from *carpal tunnel syndrome* in both hands. The third case was a 28-year-old hairdresser with abrasions and a yeast infection in her fingernails. She worked irregular hours at home in a 12-square-meter room with a small fan. She almost never washed her hands after using hair cosmetics. Other case studies indicated neuropathy after more than 20 years of pesticide spraying, allergic contact dermatitis associated with the detergent used in dish-washing, back injury after selling groceries for 18 years, and asthma in a seamstress (Sulistomo, 1997).

People in the Bandung shoemaking community felt that work safety and health had had much lower political value compared to gender and child labor issues. This lack of resources increased the public's frustration. Here are three viewpoints to illustrate this:

> May I tell you the truth, in my opinion, the government doesn't care about the OSH problem because they are very busy with their existence.

> The government doesn't care. Very few people care. When the majority of people don't care about it, then you are in a difficult position. There is no parity—no fair competition.

> Nobody cares. Nobody forbids anyone to use chemicals, nobody tells anybody about chemicals, and nobody helps.

REFLECTIONS FROM THE PHILIPPINES

Philippine Work Safety and Health Infrastructure

In the Philippines, the two principle safety and health laws are (a) the Constitution (1987) and (b) the Labor Code (1974). Both promulgate the state's responsibility to protect workers. Article XIII of the Constitution, addresses protections for women workers:

> The State shall protect working women by providing safe and healthful working conditions, taking into account their maternal functions, and such facilities and opportunities that will enhance their welfare and enable them to realize their full potential in the service of the nation. (Source: Chan Robbels Virtual Law Library)

Article 162 of the Labor Code describes OSH Standards that were formulated in 1978 and amended in 1989. Book III of the Labor Code, titled *Working Condition for Special Groups of Employees*, contains specific provisions for women and young workers (DOLE, 2001). The Department of Labor and Employment (DOLE) has primary responsibility for OSH policy and enforcement. Four DOLE units are responsible for OSH administration: (a) the Bureau of Working Conditions (BWC), (b) the aforementioned OSH Center, (c) the Employees' Compensation Commission, and (d) DOLE's 15 Regional Offices.[6] In addition, DOLE coordinates the National OSH Inter-Agency Committee. Within DOLE, a Bureau of Women and Young Workers promotes equality in employment opportunities and treatment.

The establishment of the OSH Center in 1992 was seen as encouraging development. The Center has initiated numerous research projects, training sessions, and health promotion activities in the formal and the informal sectors. But, responsibilities for health and safety are spread across ten government departments, leading to a great deal of inefficiency in monitoring and enforcement (Tescon, 2002). This is especially the case in the provinces where a lack of facilities hampers proper work environment monitoring, training, and information dissemination. Therefore, OSH remains regarded as a costly expense by enterprises. This thwarts efforts to promote hazard prevention, engineering controls, training, and outreach.

The Philippines labor force numbered more than 34.2 million in 2003 (DOLE, 2003). According to the ILO's Decent Work country report the labor force is growing by more than 2.8% a year (ILO, 2002). In 1998, there were 5,298 work-related accidents reported by 280 establishments to DOLE

---

[6]Source: In-depth interviews with several DOLE officers, in 2002.

(Tescon, 2002). Agriculture ranked the highest with 2,049 cases, followed by manufacturing with 1,659 and construction with 1,123 cases (Tescon, 2002). In 1998, disabling injuries caused 144,600 lost work days, at a cost of 10.3 million Philippine pesos (less than $200,000 United States). In 2000, there were 69,208 recorded nonagricultural occupational injuries in establishments employing 20 or more workers. There were 178 fatal injuries in this category (ILO, 2002). The 2000 National Statistics Office and the ILO Household Survey on Occupational Accidents revealed that most accidents occurred in enterprises with fewer than 20 workers (ILO, 2002).

The Bureau of Working Conditions (BWC) formulates policies and standards based on recommendations from the OSH Center and the National Inter-Agency Committee. It also monitors nationwide law enforcement. The regional DOLE offices have worksite safety and health inspection authority. The OSH Center conducts research.

In 2002, about 253 OSH inspectors were supposed to cover 820,000 workplaces. In 1989, there were about the same number of inspectors to cover 350,000 enterprises. There are approximately 700 safety officers in enterprises, though the needs estimate called for at least 54,000 officers (Tescon, 2002). Punishments for safety violations are alleged to be too lenient; as of year 2002, no employer had been jailed for OSH violations (Tescon, 2002). A forced stoppage by the government is a typical reprimand for safety and health law violations. A DOLE officer I interviewed stated:

> When we computed or estimated the number of safety officers required for the 820,000 establishments here in the Philippines, the number would be around 54,000 full-time safety officers. But there are only 700 safety officers accredited by the Bureau of Working Conditions. (DOLE officer, interviewed in Manila)

The standards needed revision, especially in the area of threshold limit values for chemicals. Where policies exist, implementation and enforcement needed to be more vigorous by DOLE and other government agencies, employers' organizations, and trade unions. While OSH administration remains fragmented, there is no clear-cut restructuring plan. One division chief of the OSH Center urged that future policies and safety and health standards needed to be more practical, thus, more enforceable for smaller businesses. The number of informal sector establishments is increasing as is the number of small enterprises. However, the majority of enterprises do not comply with OSH standards at all:

> While the OSH Standards are the (Labor) Code that is being enforced by the DOLE and concerned agency, if we pose the question of how

many enterprises are adopting or implementing OSH Standards, (we would realize that) only the big ones are fully complying with these standards. And the number, in terms of percentage, is not even 5 percent of the total number of enterprises. If we say that only five percent are complying with the OSH Standards and there are only 250 labor inspectors enforcing these standards; then we continue with such directions, it doesn't make sense at all, because we are not focusing our efforts on the bulk of the enterprises, which are the small enterprises and the informal sector enterprises. (OSH Center Division Chief, interviewed in Manila)

State inspectors are mainly assigned to inspect formal sector companies. It is the local inspectors who are in the best position to monitor safety and health at the homeworkers' and family businesses' work areas. A senior officer of the Department of Environment and Natural Resources (DENR) raised the possibility of joint-inspections as did a trade union organizer:

Maybe it's about time to operationalize joint inspection teams. Workers are prepared to take on these responsibilities. And perhaps the government and even the employers should once and for all agree to this joint inspection mechanism because you have before you well informed and trained personnel who are ready to take on this role. And it is just a matter of really calling us, and together formulate a mechanism to operationalize this inspection approach. And also, if we go into the right to know, to the labeling, etc., we need to make sure that the proper regulations are enforced. (a trade union organizer, interviewed in Manila)

An OSH Center division chief pointed out that there were no penalties or insurance premium increases for companies with hazardous working conditions. At the time of the interviews, all firms contributed to the Employees Compensation premium, at 1% of the salary of their workers. The group discussion revealed that a too small budget was appropriated for programs like the DOLE when compared to other government departments. Budget allocations illustrated the government priorities like national defense and trade and industry. Even within the DOLE, the BWC is among the lowest budgeted bureaus:

While the Philippine Constitution mandates that it is the responsibility of the state to provide humane workplace for everyone, I guess, it is not what the national leadership would like to focus on. So when we say that safety and health is the low priority among workplaces, we can look at it on a more holistic way: what are the priorities at the national agencies? (OSHA Center Division Chief, interviewed in Manila)

Informal Sector Work Environment

Invisibility Dilemma

The former Undersecretary of Labor, Ms. Lucita Lazo, described the intellectual and practical challenge in *"cracking the nut of informality."* It took time to establish a conceptual framework and strategies. It was difficult to confront the notion that the informal sector was disappearing. Lazo explained:

> . . . it is pretty clear now—invisibility, lack of access to productive resources, lack of access to social protection, and safety nets. They (informal sector workers) are not counted by official statistics because there is no definition for them. From there, because there is no statistics on them, they are not part of a policy, they are not part of planning. Therefore there is no program, no budget, consequently, no service—a whole vicious chain, which people don't seem to realize. You know the policy-makers would even say "why are you spending (time) on definition?" Definition can be as crucial as anything can be, because when you start enumerating them in statistics you have to begin with the definition. (Ms. Lazo, interviewed in Manila)

A trade union organizer discussed the "invisibility dilemma" but indicated that the country was beginning to define the sector:

> The project with TUCP is now heading towards occupational safety and health. Before, OSH was never given attention. It was almost ignored by policy-makers. I learned so many things from my experience in empowering women and homeworkers—especially on whom really to address and why there are no specific programs for the informal sector. And the usual response to us by the policy-makers is that they do not know where we are—our invisibility. So in the present advocacy, we make it sure that we will be able to define from the Philippine perspective what an informal sector is. So last week, the National Statistical Coordination Board has passed a resolution defining the informal sector in the country. So maybe we are the first to define the sector. (Female trade-union organizer, interviewed in Manila)

Social Protection

For the informal sector, social protection must be viewed broadly. Western countries construe social protection as insurance where revenue is pooled from taxation system. Also, employers and workers pay in and establish a fund which covers injured workers. The informal sector is more challenging and Lazo suggested that such insurance programs needed a local base. Nevertheless, any social protection programs needed revenue. But for Lazo, these should not come solely from the state:

There has to be some form of subsidization from the state and, in fact, the path I have taken in respect to that is to look at what we call indigenous or local schemes. In the past, traditionally, in the Philippines, when somebody dies, the hat is passed around literally, and somebody contributes and (with) that we are able to cover the burial cost. So why not simply build from these local practices and make them the building block for a social protection scheme. It doesn't even have to be a national scheme. It could be a community-based scheme.

. . . even what you call "safety net" "social protection," if you look at it in the light of our economic situation now, it is very hard to rationalize because you have a country that has a huge deficit. Where will it draw the money for subsidies? Scheme should not be purely subsidized. It has to be contributory—the worker has to have a stake in it, no matter how small his or her contribution is—there has to be an equity coming from the worker. (Ms. Lazo)

With just 28% of the formal sector labor force covered by the Social Security System, one can see the difficulties in covering informal sector workers (PhilHealth Statistics, 2001). Rural and urban informal sector workers remain uncovered. PhilHealth—the Philippine Health Insurance Agency—has made some efforts, but its funds are insufficient. From January to June 2002, PhilHealth paid about 64% to the private sector (including individually paying members), 33% to the government sector, and less than 3% to indigenous members. Civil society groups, cooperatives, community-based organizations, and some trade unions are trying to help their members access social protection services, through such efforts as community-based micro insurance schemes (PhilHealth Statistics, 2001).

There are some positive developments in funding community health insurance schemes. Aviva Ron compared rural community health insurance programs in the Philippines and Guatemala. She described how programs were organized by the Mother and Child Care Community Based Integrated Project (MCC) in La Union Province of the Philippines (Ron, 1999). It utilized an approach developed by the international NGO *Organization for Education Resources and Training* (ORT) and offered basic health care as a major component (Ron, 1999). The National Health Insurance Law (1995) was to provide a universal health care benefit package. Ron estimated that such coverage could take at least 15 years to reach rural communities. Meanwhile community initiatives are encouraged. In just three years the MCC-ORT scheme provided health care affordable and accessible to 3,000 low income families (Ron, 1999). The local cooperative provided the administrative structure for the health care team which provided ambulatory and inpatient care as well as prescribed drugs (Ron, 1999).

Safety and Health

The OSH Center and the Institute of Labor Studies (ILS) jointly studied, monitored, and interacted with informal sector workers in four occupations: battery recycling, metal fabrication, sugar cane harvesting, and woodworking. The two institutions published a monograph of their findings (ILS & OSHC, 1999). Among the studied four groups, safety and health hazards formed a long list: poor housekeeping; pressured gas tanks in the work areas and other fire and explosion hazards; noise, heat, and humidity; welding without protective equipment; electric shocks; fumes from organic solvents; exposure to sulfuric acid; smoke (CO, ashes, soot) from burning sugar cane fields; wood, soil, and metal dusts; prolonged sitting, standing, bending, and squatting; carrying too heavy loads; and stagnant water breeding mosquitoes (ILS & OSHC, 1999). Medical examinations revealed multiple health effects, including elevated lead and leukocyte levels in the blood, corneal burns from flying welding sparks, tool cuts, decreased lung function, musculoskeletal disorders, and symptoms of communicable diseases (ILS & OSHC, 1999).The joint study team determined that it would be unrealistic to enforce formal sector health and safety regulations in the informal sector. Instead, it recommended advocacy and education rather than punishment and sanctions (ILS & OSHC, 1999). A senior officer at the DENR I interviewed also cautioned about excessive restrictions. Too much control on informal sector workers would make them shift to another industry or activity or hide their work activities. Poor people are usually intimidated and harassed by enforcement authorities (National Anti-Poverty Commission, 1998).

In my interviews, I tried to discover reasons why OSH is deprioritized. According to Lazo, day-to-day survival is a legitimate concern among the poorest of the poor: workplace health and safety appear less important, however it is not their conscious intent to downgrade safety. In the interview, she noted that at the International Conference of Women in Beijing (1995) western delegates wanted to discuss violence against women. A woman from a developing country, while she did not disagree with the importance of the topic noted that the problems in developed countries appeared remote to women in developing countries concerned with finding clean water to drink and food for their children.

ORGANIZING INFORMAL SECTOR WORKERS

There are global and national women's movements that have managed to organize informal sector workers. The Self-Employed Women's Association (SEWA), Ahmedabad, India, is perhaps the most lively such alliance. The government of India has even asked SEWA's representatives to participate in a process to formulate a national policy on home-based work (Chen, 2001). SEWA has been a founding member of HomeNET for home-based workers, StreetNet for street vendors, as well as WIEGO, which has affiliates in more than 21 countries as well as project partners and activities in more than a dozen countries (Chen, 1999, 2001). SEWA was also pioneering the ILO's Home Work Convention. In its essence, WIEGO is an international research and policy analysis network concentrating on poor workers in the informal economy, especially women. In 1994, members of various grassroots organizations formed HomeNet to support the development of organizations for homeworkers and to improve working and living conditions for home-based workers worldwide. Both WIEGO and HomeNet have extensive constituencies, therefore, ideal at raising awareness and communicating about work-related hazards and working conditions in general. Women garment homeworkers in Bulacan, the Philippines, formed a pre-cooperative and held a series of consultative dialogues leading to the formation of the Philippine national women's homeworker organization and network called PATAMABA (Pidena-Ofreneo, 1993).

CONCLUSION

This chapter has overviewed key characteristics of the informal sector. Structural adjustment policies, feeble legal structures, and general political unattractiveness are all reasons that produce low budget allocations for public efforts like building up OSH infrastructure. Inefficient workplace inspections and their follow-ups are examples of manifestations of a weak OSH infrastructure. Both countries had decentralized their inspection authorities at the regional level, but it was particularly at the regional level where minuscule resources were allocated for enforcement, research, and advocacy.

At the end, we may ask ourselves whether it is unrealistic to anticipate formalization of the informal at least to the extent where workers would not only struggle to survive but live on with decent jobs? The organizing success stories of SEWA, WIEGO, PATAMABA, and others show that solutions may not be that complicated provided there is political will and support from the government (Chen, 2001; Chen et al., 2002; Pidena-Ofreneo, 1993; WIEGO, 2003).

REFERENCES

Achmadi, U., & Wibisana, W. (1997). The primary health care-based occupational health care delivery system—Experience from Indonesia. In *The proceedings of International Conference on Occupational Health Safety in the Informal Sector.* The Department of Health, Indonesia, pp. 49-57.

Asian Development Bank (ADB). (2002). Country economic review: Indonesia. ADB, Manila, p.5. Retrieved at: http://www.adb.org/Documents/CERs/INO/2003/default.asp

Carnoy, M. (1999). The family, flexible workforce and social cohesion at risk. *International Labor Review, 138*(4), 411-429.

Chan Robbels Virtual Law Library. Constitution of the Philippines. (1987). http://www.chanrobles.com/philsupremelaw.htm

Chen, M. A. (1999). The invisible workforce: Women in the informal economy. *International Perspectives on Work and the Economy, 1*(1). Radcliffe Public Policy Center, the Harvard University, Cambridge, MA.

Chen, M. A. (2001). Women in the informal sector: A global picture, the global movement. *SAIS Review, 21*(1), 71-82.

Chen, M. A., Jhabvala, R., & Lund, F. (2002). Supporting workers in the informal economy: A policy framework. International Labour Office (ILO). Employment Sector Working Paper on the Informal Economy. Retrieved at: http://www.wiego.org/papers/ilo_wp2.pdf

Dagg, A. (1996). Organizing homeworkers into unions. In E. Boris & E. Prûgl (Eds.), *Homeworkers in global perspective: Invisible no more* (pp. 239-258). New York: Routledge.

Department of Health, Indonesia. (2002). *Strategic Planning of Occupational Health Program 2002-2004.* Jakarta: Department of Health.

Department of Labor and Employment (DOLE), the Philippines. (2003). *Key labor and employment statistics.* Manila: DOLE. Retrieved at: http://www.dole.gov.ph

Department of Labor and Employment (DOLE), the Philippines. (2001). Occupational Safety and Health Standards (as amended). The Bureau of Working Conditions. Manila: DOLE.

Department of Manpower and Transmigration (DEPNAKER). (1996). Regulation of the Department of Manpower and Transmigration, No: PER.05/MEN/1996, Occupational Safety and Health Management System. Department of Manpower and Transmigration, Jakarta.

De Soto, H. (2000). *The mystery of capital: Why capitalism triumphs in the West and fails everywhere else* (pp. 12, 21, 93, 207). New York: Basic Books.

De Soto, H. (1989). *The other path: The economic answer to terrorism* (pp. xxiii-xxv). New York: Basic Books.

Heikel, M. V. (2000). Homeworkers in Paraguay. International Labour Office. *Boosting Employment Through Small Enterprise Development (SEED).* Working Paper No. 2. Retrieved at: http://www.ilo.org/dyn/infoecon/docs/296/F92134100/Homework%20in%20 Paraguay.pdf

Hennon, C. B., Locker, S., & Walker, R. (2000). *Gender and home-based employment.* London, UK: Auburn House.

Institute of Labor Studies (ILS), and Occupational Safety and Health Center (OSHC). (1999). A closer look into the working conditions and occupational safety and health of informal sector workers: A compilation of case studies.

Monograph Series No. 11. Department of Labor and Employment (DOLE), the Philippines.

International Labour Office (ILO). (1991). The dilemma of the informal sector. Report of the Director-General. International Labour Conference, 78th Session. ILO, Geneva.

International Labour Office (ILO). (1996). Homework Convention (No. 177, 1996). ILO, Geneva. Retrieved at: http://ilolex.ilo.ch:1567/english/convdisp2.htm

International Labour Office (ILO). (2002a). *Decent work and the informal economy.* International Labour Conference, 90th Session. Geneva: ILO. Retrieved at: http://www.ilo.org/public/libdoc/ilo/2002/102B09_133_engl.pdf

International Labour Office (ILO). (2002b). Employment Sector. 2002. *Women and men in the informal economy: A statistical picture The Global Workforce: A Statistical Picture* (pp. 6-7). Geneva: ILO.

International Labour Office (ILO). (2002c). *Action programme for decent work: The Philippines.* Manila: ILO. South-East Asia Multidisciplinary Advisory Team.

Joedoatmodjo, S. (1999). Occupational safety and health for the informal sector: Seeking better solutions for Indonesia.

National Anti-Poverty Commission, the Philippines. (1998). Sectoral Assemblies: Participants reference documents.

Occupational Health Center, Indonesia. (2002). *Warta Kesehta Kerja. Media Komunikasi Kesehatan Kerja*, Edition 1, (Indonesian language). Department of Health, Jakarta.

PhilHealth Statistics. (2002). Philippine Health Insurance Corporation.

Pidena-Ofreneo, R. (1993). Garments homeworkers in Bulacan. In L. Lazo (Ed.), *From the shadows to the fore: Practical actions for the social protection of homeworkers in the Philippines* (pp. 1-32). International Labour Office (ILO), Bangkok.

Prügl, E. (1999). *The global construction of gender: Home-based work in the political economy of the 20th century.* New York: Columbia University Press.

Prügl, E., & Tinker, I. (1997). Microentrepreneurs and homeworkers: Convergent categories. *World Development, 25*(9), 1471-1482.

Ron, A. (1999). NGOs in community health insurance schemes: Examples from Guatemala and the Philippines. *Social Science and Medicine, 48,* 939-950.

Rudjito. (2002). *Strategies for developing micro, small, and medium enterprises (MSME).* International Visitor Program. Bank Rakyat, Indonesia. Retrieved at: http://www.asli.com.my/documents/msme.pdf

State Gazette of the Republic of Indonesia. Act of the Republic of Indonesia, Number 13 Year 2003, Concerning Manpower (unofficial English translation).

Sulistomo, A. (1997). Case studies on health problems of women working in the informal sector in Jakarta and it's surroundings. In *The proceedings of International Conference on Occupational Health Safety in the Informal Sector* (pp. 160-166). The Department of Health, Indonesia.

Susilastuti, D. H. (1996). Home-based work as a rural survival strategy. In E. Boris & E. Prûgl (Eds.), *Homeworkers in global perspective: Invisible no more* (pp. 129-142). New York: Routledge.

Taufiqurrahman, M. (2003). Local companies negligent about workers' safety. *The Jakarta Post,* January 10, 2003.

Taufiqurrahman, M., & Unidjaja, F. D. (2003). Companies must improve workers' safety: Mega. *The Jakarta Post,* January 14, 2003.

Tate, J. (1996). Making links. In E. Boris & E. Prûgl (Eds.), *Homeworkers in global perspective: Invisible no more* (pp. 273-290). New York: Routledge.

Tecson, A. (2002). *Country report: Philippines.* Presentation during the Training on Green Productivity. Occupational Safety and Health Center of the Philippines, Department of Labor and Employment (DOLE).

Tokman, V. (2001). Integrating the informal sector into the modernization process. *SAIS Review, 21*(1), 45-60.

Tomei, M. (2000). *Home work in selected Latin American countries: A comparative view.* International Labour Office (ILO). Boosting employment through small enterprise development (SEED). Working paper No. 1.

Topobroto, H. S. (2002). *Policy and condition of occupational safety and health in Indonesia.* International Labour Office (ILO), Jakarta.

The Jakarta Post. (2002). Occupational accident rate remains high. September 17, 2002.

Wooding, J., & Levenstein, C. (1999). The point of production: Work environment in advanced industrial societies. New York: The Guilford Press.

Women in Informal Employment Globalizing and Organizing (WIEGO). (2003). *Addressing informality, reducing poverty: A policy response to the informal economy.* A policy booklet. WIEGO, Carr Center for Human Rights, Harvard University, Cambridge, MA and Gender and Youth Affairs Division, Commonwealth Secretariat, London (sponsor). Available at: http://www.wiego.org/publications/policybooklet.pdf

CHAPTER 4

Does Gender Matter?

> When employment activities take place in one's dwelling, it brings
> paid work into the space where duty, need, and love motivate the labor.
> Home-based employment helps to construct gender at the household
> level. (Hennon & Loker, 2000)

Gender within the social relations of economic globalization has important
implications for the health and social welfare of both sexes. For analytical and
ethical reasons I believe that the gender topic itself requires special attention.
I am particularly interested in this for various reasons, including:

- the disruption of the traditional household by an invasive global market
  capitalism affects physical, mental, social health of women and their
  families. The informal sector within the context of globalization has provided me with an excellent ground on which to examine gender issues;
- women may be subject to "super-exploitation" because of the cultural
  gender roles, hence, traditional women's inferior position in the social
  hierarchies;
- gender still remains only vaguely discussed by occupational safety and
  health (OSH) practitioners and professionals;
- traditional or modern methods of political participation—trade unions,
  political parties, and non-government organizations (NGOs)—may not
  be as open to women in developing countries who therefore may be
  without their own voice or that of an advocate in political discussions
  affecting them; and
- the fact that I am a woman plays a role in my interest and empathy for
  the problems of women.

ECONOMIC GLOBALIZATION AND IMPACT ON WOMEN'S HEALTH AND WELL-BEING

A wealth of studies focuses on globalization's impacts on women. The global urge for locating cheap labor has been dismantling the traditional social support networks, cultural norms, and welfare systems (Hartigan, Price, & Tolhurst, 2002). An emphasis on private property and commercialization marginalized women's access to vital social resources and basic needs such as health and education (Sen & Grown, 1987). Pyle determined major factors in the deterioration of the quality of women's lives in developing countries including an export-driven development strategy that places importance on multi-national corporations, subcontracting practices, establishing export processing zones, and hiring homeworkers for higher production and rates (Pyle, 1999, 2001). Home is an ideal sphere to investigate how gender shapes labor—paid and unpaid, visible and invisible—and although homeworkers have employment they might otherwise not have, it can be argued that they are being exploited for the benefit of others, both capitalists and consumers for lower priced goods (Hennon & Loker, 2000). Moran's *Beyond Sweatshops* elaborated women's lower salaries in the factories in developing countries: while wage discrepancies may sometimes reflect lower productivity and skill levels, survey evidence shows that young women are paid less simply because they are more passive and docile than male workers (Moran, 2002). Some employers justified the lower wage rates for women by contending that women require no more than a supplement to the main family income because they are not breadwinners (Elson, 1983; Moran, 2002).

Structural adjustment programs (SAPs)—fostered by the global financial institutions—brought along significant gendered health impacts by cutting public expenditures that weakened social, health, and education sectors (Standing, 2002). In the health sector, these cost cuts can be perceived as reduced services and maintenance, missing or broken equipment, and facilities in poor condition (Standing, 2002). Deterioration of reproductive health services affects women disproportionally, yet, women are mostly the ones who take care of children, dependents, and sick family members (Standing, 2002). Because of introduced fees and restrained budgets, pregnant women stop seeking care, hospitals cannot offer treatment for the poor, and people die of preventable causes because drugs and trained providers are not available (Bangser, 2002).

GENDER WITHIN OCCUPATIONAL SAFETY AND HEALTH (OSH)

Gender inequity influences the work environment and therefore OSH. Nevertheless, OSH activities are very often gender insensitive. In the past, only men's work was considered real work—and still is by many societies. That fact has been made clear by a host of scholars and advocates. Women's work was viewed as secondary, not real work at all. Women's work hazards have received little attention, hence work-related health consequences are under-researched (Messing, 2002; Messing, Dumais, & Romito, 1993; Stellman, 1982). Gender segregation at work is an important starting point for identifying women's and men's OSH concerns. Labor markets are sex segregated; women and men perform different jobs and are exposed to different hazards. Within the same job title, women and men may be assigned different tasks (Messing, Punnett, Bond, Alexanderson, Pyle, Zahn, et al., 2003).

Several factors influence chemical exposures of female workers: (a) women's bodies contain more fat tissue than men's, thus, they are at greater risk of harm from solvent exposures; (b) there are gender differences in the absorption, metabolism, and excretion of solvents—because women have slower metabolism than men, chemicals remain in women's bloodstreams longer; and (c) women have thinner skin than men, so their bodies more easily absorb chemicals through the skin and cause allergies and other skin disorders (Östlin, 2002). Exposure limits for hazardous substances are determined based on the case of healthy young men, with the exposure limits then adapted for female workers, without the evidence about how they would affect women (Östlin, 2002). When protective regulations (e.g., against reproductive hazards) and other measures are introduced, they tend to eliminate women from jobs or marginalize their tasks rather than eliminate the exposures from women's work (Messing, 2002; Messing, Dumais, & Romito, 1993; Quinn, Woskie, & Rosenberg, 2000).

Messing and a group of occupational and gender specialists stated that it is true that men die and get injured traumatically on the job more often than women, but women's jobs are more likely to lead to chronic slowly developing conditions, in particular, those that emerge from poor ergonomics design (Messing et al., 2003). Indeed, a plethora of ergonomic risk factors and psychosocial hazards are found in women's work environment: repetitive and monotonous tasks, stress, part-time jobs, little authority, and violence (Östlin, 2002; Quinn et al., 2000). Karasek's demand-control model analysis indicates that women are mostly concentrated in high-strain jobs, characterized by high psychosocial demands as well as low control and authority over how to carry out the job tasks (Karasek & Theorell, 1990). Wooding and Levenstein estimate that in the United States, an average working woman spends 80 hours a week on both job and household work and up to 105 hours if she has sole responsibility for her children. An average man spends about 10 hours a week on household tasks (Wooding & Levenstein, 1999). The wage gap remains the chief socio-economic gender discrepancy (Quinn et al., 2000). In 2002, average earnings for women in the United States were 73 cents for every dollar earned by men (Messing et al., 2003). The work sex segregation is a chief factor determining male-female wage differences and women are entering to non-traditional jobs in increasing numbers (Quinn et al., 2000). Nonetheless, women's entry to conventional male jobs has often been stifled on the basis of their supposed biological differences: they are presumed to be weaker and technically less adept than men (Messing, Doniol-Shaw, & Haëntjens, 1994).

REFLECTIONS FROM INDONESIA

Women's Occupational Safety and Health (OSH)

In Indonesia, women's OSH has been largely overlooked by programs that focus on reproductive health issues and while women's OSH is neglected, greater resources are allocated to OSH programs that impact men (Brogan, 1994). Melody Kemp's work has revealed how OSH-related laws, regulations, and technical standards in Indonesia and elsewhere define protection from a male perspective. The Indonesian Work Safety Act (1970) has been written in such a way that it relates more to working men than working women. Furthermore, in Indonesia, the government department in charge of labor issues is called the Department of Manpower and the nation's recent labor law is called the Manpower Act. When companies establish OSH committees they are typically made up of men, even in workplaces where women predominate (e.g., the garment sector) even though it is precisely through service on these committees where women can become dynamic, act as organizers, and influence work safety and health (Kemp, 2002).

Gender and OSH have been topics at the Indonesian Tripartite OSH Council. A Council member noted in an interview how Indonesian culture still segregates the labor market and economy. By the same token, he thought that the Indonesian gender movement is strong:

> . . . once in here in an official meeting, I raised a question whether it is wise to (allow) women workers to work in the underground mining, so four ladies—two on my right and two on my left—picked so hard: "Women can work everywhere!" Ok, ok. We love women, why should they work in an underground mine? But they like that. They go everywhere. The government asked me about the gender issue. I thought they can work everywhere, but not in the very dangerous area. But the women members said: "No matter, we can work everywhere, everyday, just agree with that. (Representative of the National Tripartite OSH Council, interviewed in Jakarta)

Social norms peeked through in my conversations even with well-educated women. When I asked women how they chose their occupations, they often answered, *"I did not choose this,"* and added that they were working in their current positions because that they had been asked to do so by their supervisors. No male informants replied this way. For men, *"there was a possibility and I applied," "this is the call of the heart,"* or it is *"my life's mission."* Medical doctors—men and women—often answered *"we are meant to help people."*

The men and women I interviewed indicated that women and children always become the victims during the hard times of economic collapse. A government officer described some NGO efforts to prevent violence against women. Among the poor, violence and bad economics are intertwined. For example:

> . . . if the family doesn't get money, the husband hits the wife because the wife has not produced the money for the family. So it relates very much with the informal sector; sometimes, they let the wife do the prostitution because of no money at home. Our Demographic Institute studies indicate that during the economic crisis years 1997-1998, many women were pushed into the prostitution. (Female government representative, interviewed in Jakarta)

As an example of globalized economic consequences on women's health, we can examine the UNDP's reports on dramatic cuts in Indonesia's public health due to the country's economic crisis. Between 1995 and 1999 the proportion of the population "without access to health services" rose from 10.6% to 21.6% (United Nations Development Programme [UNDP], 2001). Public expenditure on health fell 8% during 1996–97 and by a further 12% during 1998–99: the proportion of adults who had used public health services, such as public clinics, in the previous month fell from 7.4% to 5.6% (UNDP, 2001). In some cases it may have been because people did not have money for any kind of health care; in others, they were simply going to private clinics. The proportion of children using health facilities dropped from 26% to 20% (UNDP, 2001).

Home-Based Business Management and Gendered Division of Labor in Shoemaking

Husbands manage and decide family business matters in most instances. During my interviews in the Jakarta area when I asked how husbands and wives shared business management responsibilities, many implied: "in principle, no objection with sharing the management responsibilities, however, we still wonder whether women can "handle tough and important situations." For example, a business representative wondered:

> . . . sometimes, if we are dealing with female management and male management, the decision can be very strict, so slow sometimes, many factors to be considered . . . Sometimes, female management is not too strong enough to make a very-very important decision. Sometimes, but not always. (A male business representative, interviewed in Jakarta)

Mr. Hakim whose wife participated in the management suggested that women indeed are "tough" and competent managers whereas men lacked precision and attention to details. He said:

> Women work in tasks which need precision, and I don't know if there is a basic nature in men that they are not precise enough. My wife works in administration because she's really competent—women are really competent in this kind of job. I share this job with my wife. I deal with the production directly, but for setting prices, that's my wife's job. I'm too kind—can't help if the customer says "please give me a lower price." I would give the customer a lower price. (Mr. Hakim, a custom-made boots manufacturer)

Not everyone denounced gender segregation. While an academic I interviewed spoke against nepotism and favoritism, in his opinion, shoe manufacturing should be dichotomized as: (a) clean work for women and (b) dirty for men. Women should not be gluing, but doing soft and clean tasks, like packaging and accounting. Men could glue, press, or grind:

> it's ok to be differentiated . . . differentiate or distinguish. It is ok, but please, based on the capacity as male or female. For instance, in the shoe industry, the male employer is better just concentrating in working, physically working to produce a shoe . . . but the female employer, it's better they're working on the packaging. . . . the female employer, involving the physical work—I don't agree with that. I always suggest to them that male and female has a different function of working at the system. (A male academic, interviewed in Bandung)

The opinion expressed above—"light-and-clean-jobs-for-women" and "heavy--and-dirty-jobs-for-men"—illustrates how deeply social norms are rooted. Manual laundry washing and house-cleaning are heavy, dirty, and dangerous jobs, but undoubtedly few men would find them so appealing that they would become exclusively their jobs. The social norms convey a silent message: heavy, dirty, and dangerous work is valued more if it is a man's work, and therefore, it pays more; woman's work is not valued so much, no matter how heavy and dirty.

Finances and Managing the Business

Wives have an important task taking care of finances and the cash the *bengkels* generate. When purchases are made, husbands ask their wives for money. In terms of shoe production, wives made the patterns on the leather, cleaned, packed, and sorted. Wives also calculated raw material costs, final selling prices and profits, and electricity costs. But "taking care of the money" does not indicate female dominance in the family. Diane Wolf reviewed several studies on women's control over income and household finances, and how it might connect to autonomy and household power (Wolf, 2000) in Central and West Java. In Central Java, 80% of the wives interviewed said that they took care of the household money. The majority said that they decided how to spend it with their husbands. In poor households, there was little extra money for the wife to spend and in West Javanese households just half the women decided on their own how to spend the money they earned (Wolf, 2000). Wolf suggests that women might manage the household account income but this needed to be distinguished from controlling decisions about expenditures.

According to Mr. Saleh, the wives of the *bengkel owners* were dominant when they managed the *tukang*s and acquired raw material. He thought that in most cases husbands shared an equal management responsibility. Mr. Iman mentioned that when he traveled, his wife stayed behind and took care of the business. Although many informants stated that work tasks were shared, in general, husbands were the major shareholders. Three different Cibaduyut viewpoints illustrated this:

> The husband is more or less the manager and he does the most . . . of course, the wives always help in finishing, putting labels, and sorting. (Mr. and Mrs. Dahn, homeworker couple, interviewed in Bandung).

> In most cases, it's the husband who is the main shareholder of the bengkel business. Sometimes, in many cases, the husbands just don't care. They care more about their hobbies: singing birds, fishing, and let the wives as another shareholder to take care of the bengkel management. But the husbands work also in the production, doing the concrete work, and letting the wives take care of money. It's possible that the wife is the main shareholder. (Mr. Annan, skilled shoe maker/organizer, interviewed in Bandung)

> . . . I'm in charge of getting orders, my brothers are in charge of the production, and my wife is in charge of the financial matters. Even

the bank account for this bengkel is on her name, my wife's name. I don't know how much money there is in the account. (Mr. Saleh, skilled shoemaker/business owner, interviewed in Bandung)

If the wife was clearly the sole manager of a bigger business, it was typically an indication that she had brought in a considerable amount of business capital (i.e., family money) from the very beginning. In these situations, the gender-based job division blurred and tasks were assigned to workers based on their skills. Nonetheless, "skills"—that is, capacity and capability—also echo the constructs of traditions and social norms and neither gender is encouraged to learn new skills, especially if the new skill is not considered "normal" for him or her in the society. Skills transmission is absent and neither gender is encouraged to learn what they do not already know. In Ms. Dessy's *bengkel*, in Indonesia, the tasks were assigned based on person's skills:

We don't consider gender as an issue here because the criteria here to do things are based on their capability and capacity. For example the son, he can't do the marketing, like going around shops and offering new models. My daughter is much better in doing that so she is in charge of that. And, my husband is good at designing so that's what he does, designs. (Ms. Dessy, business owner)

Yes, husbands and wives work in the bengkels, but their roles and tasks depend on their skill. . . . When a man and a woman get married, it's a kind of a business joint venture as well. If the husband has some money and the wife also has some too, then, they are shareholders of the bengkel . . . to clarify the marriage joint-venture statement, it's not the main motivation to get married. People get married because they like each other. But it often happens here that the husband has the skill and knowledge to produce shoes and the bride has the money. Why not to set up a bengkel? (Mr. Annan, skilled shoe maker/organizer, interviewed in Bandung)

Why Aren't Women Skilled Shoemakers?

Female skilled shoemakers (*tukangs*) were rare in Bandung. I wanted to find out why. According to one shoemaker, women were not confident being *tukangs*. He added that he would not trust women *tukangs* because it was men's work. For him, women making shoes was a funny idea. Second shoemaker thought that I was being humorous with my question and exclaimed that "*I think from that corner until the monument there, you will not find one.*" A third person said that he had seen women *tukangs*. A woman can be a *tukang,* but the work atmosphere was tough; men used rough language and women would most likely feel uncomfortable working with them.

Household Duties and Child Care

Though household task-sharing exists, men are considered to be the main breadwinners. In Indonesia, wives raise children, cook, and sometimes may get involved in the management of the *bengkel*. They sometimes bring their children along to the *bengkel*. When wives do not want to cook, families eat out or buy food from *warung*.[1] Sometimes, husbands help with household tasks like washing heavy clothes. Mrs. Dessy asserted that everyone in her family shared responsibilities. If she is busy and her husband is at home at meal time, then her husband is responsible for providing food. One husband described Cibaduyut women as "smarter than men" and noted that many big stores are managed by women.

But, in general, traditional roles and practices remain intact. Below are two answers to a question regarding the sharing of household responsibilities in Indonesia:

> Of course the wives are also involved in the bengkel business but at home they are housewives. When it is time to cook, then they cook; if it is time to take care of children, they take care of children. Husbands never cook (laughing). Only wives. (Mr. Hiet, retired shoemaker and business owner, interviewed in Bandung)

> My wife is fully in charge of the household matters and I'm fully in charge of my business. It's been changing a little bit the situation now because shoe shops normally trust women more. (Mr. Ari, skilled shoe-maker (tukang), interviewed in Bandung)

Because women are mothers, they were believed to have a natural platform to contribute to the community health via household management. While welcoming women to participate in community safety, health, and environmental activities is encouraging, it is vital to avoid confining women's participation to a caretaker role for the sick (Sen & Grown, 1987). An academic's viewpoint illustrates women's role in building the community health:

> I think it has slightly changed, the man is also taking care of the children but still that woman plays more (role) than a man here in Indonesia. That's why a woman can play also an important role in health. Women know children better than a man. They know why they have health ailments . . .

---

[1] *Warung*, Indonesian term, means a trolley where food is sold and served to the customers.

because the mothers, at least, will be taking care of their own children. And then, from taking care of their own children, they will be taking care of other children. A woman can play an important role, because a woman can warn the husband and other people about the dangerous things. (A male academic, interviewed in Bandung)

REFLECTIONS FROM THE PHILIPPINES

A division chief of the OSH Center described the multiple burdens placed on women workers. Women bear multiple burdens in the informal and formal economies that become accentuated in home-based business management. Women market and sell the products, manage the staff, cook for the family, clean the house, mind and teach their children, and take care of the laundry. Women who are able to cope with these multiple burdens are usually assisted by other family members or in rare instances their company provides day care facilities. Sexual and general harassment are a constant problem. The director of the OSH Center noted:

> Even in very articulate societies such as ours, women are very artic-
> ulate, open, but they are still harassed. (Director of the OSH Center,
> interviewed in Manila)

I did witness a refreshing polar opposite from the typical sex segregated labor market. Women outnumbered men in government leadership and technical specialist positions. Women were especially well represented in the government safety inspectorate where they outnumbered men. This is despite the fact that the Labor Code refers to safety *man,* not to safety *officer.* Such terminology is consciously and subconsciously mirrored in the workplace. A division chief of the OSH Center described it:

> A few days ago, I received a call from a female worker asking me the
> question: "is it necessary that a safety and health officer be a male?"
> Taking off from her question, it seems that there is still a notion among
> workplaces that a safety engineer or a safety officer has to be a male. It
> could be that among workplaces, they still give priority to male safety
> engineers (over female safety engineers). It could still be the situation.
> (A division chief of the OSH Center, interviewed in Manila)

Notwithstanding, in the Bureau of Working Conditions (BWC) and in the OSH Center, more women than men occupy professional and technical positions. During my visit, three out of four BWC divisions were led by women. At the OSH Center, four out of five division chiefs were women as were the executive director and the deputy director were female. These observations were corroborated by the UNDP's Gender Empowerment Measure which considers the share of women in parliament, managerial and professional positions, and their income compared to men (UNDP, 2003). Out of 70 countries evaluated by the UNDP, the Philippines was ranked 35. Seventeen percent of parliament seats are held by women, 35% of managers and administrators are female, and 66% of professional and technical workers are women (UNDP, 2003). Nonetheless, wage gaps are large; women earn 69 pesos for every 100 pesos earned by a man (UNDP, 2003).

The role of the religion was raised. Two trade-unionists discussed the impact of the Catholic Church on work gender segregation and health promotion:

> We have a priest who is a man. Women would always be just assisting them as nuns, etc. I think religion has really played a big role in shaping our minds, especially in the gender divisions of labor and I think it continues . . . because even the women activists would say "women have rights!" but when you really go down and ask grassroots women, . . . they would always say the opposite of what the women activists were expressing. There is a disparity. (A trade-union representative, interviewed in Manila)

> In Catholic-dominated places, people would usually disagree with us in the campaign for reproductive health or campaign for population control. They are always against us. They are more for the traditional role of women. That's why there is a big need to educate our women in the communities. (Another trade-union representative, interviewed in Manila)

The Catholic Church plays a pivotal role in various health promotion activities. Besides reproductive health, condom use in HIV/AIDS prevention has been a target of fierce debate. Since women's extraordinary presence in high leadership positions of work life was palpable in the capital area, one would assume that women's empowerment must have penetrated into all levels of the society in many areas. This was not the case and it is evident that the Catholic Church plays a major role in molding the traditional social norms in rural areas. As one of the interviewees mentioned: *"The president of the Republic of the Philippines can be a woman—but the priest of the Catholic Church is a man."* Globally, major religious institutions have a profound influence on advocacy everywhere.

Home-Based Business Management and Gendered Division of Labor in Shoemaking

People I interviewed described men's and women's roles in home-based business management. According to the former Undersecretary of Labor, small home-based enterprises are typically managed by women; larger firms are run by men.

> When it (enterprise) gets bigger, the men come into the picture and start becoming presidents of the company. When it is small, the woman does everything, from marketing to production, to the day-to-day record-ing—that's the woman's area. But when the business grows and starts blooming, the man would come into the picture. (Ms. Lazo, interviewed in Manila)

A trade union organizer noted that in home-based firms men are the opera-tions managers while women handle the finances and clerical responsibilities.

> . . . the man is manning the operation. They control the operation. But the women sit on the table, compute money, doing orders, calculations, and all that. It's a set up for them. It's the women who are doing the clerical jobs and accounting. Even the children, girls usually help the mother in the calculations and the boys are doing the operations. So that's usually how it is in the family business. (A female trade-union representative, interviewed in Manila)

A second trade union organizer confirmed that men are regarded as in-charge of firms while women handle the finances in a more subordinate role.

> So it is more of the men making the decisions and the women making sure that the decisions of the men are implemented. Women are the secretaries, the finance persons in the business undertaking. I think they are more relegated to these roles. But there has been a movement towards women also taking part in the decision-making process in business estab-lishments. This is actually a growing movement now with the women empowerment and gender development slowly getting into the conscious-ness of the Filipinos. Women are getting involved in decision-making, direct running of the businesses. (Male trade-union representative, interviewed in Manila)

There is a clear gendered division of labor in shoe manufacturing. Women prepare upper shoe parts while men put upper and lower footwear pieces together. Because the men's job is considered more difficult and more impor-tant they earn more than women. Women also often clean the shoes. The wife in one family folded boxes and cleaned and polished shoes. Sometimes, a husband earns primary income elsewhere. For example, one husband worked as a driver for their subcontractor.

Husbands and wives may share tasks. Mr. and Mrs. Francis said that when either of them is out running errands, the other took charge of everything.

Mrs. Francis negotiated with subcontractors and managers. She also purchased raw materials and delivered finished shoes. Mr. Francis lifted and carried heavy loads. They did the accounting together. Mr. Francis explained that normally men took care of the raw material acquisitions and production while women handled the finances.

In Mrs. and Mr. Eno's (subcontractors) family, the husband reported he and his wife worked together. Mrs. Eno took care of the store in Baclaran with the help of one of their children. The husband loaded shoes into the van and transported them around the area. However, Mrs. Eno stated:

> But I'm the one managing the business, dealing with suppliers and customers. My husband does not deal with them. I told him it's wrong. It's different when he knows how to deal with them. When you say women of Biñan it means industrious, when you say men of Biñan it means indolent. But my husband is kind. Industrious men are rare. In 100 men, maybe only 10 are industrious.

Mrs. Lane (another subcontractor) commented that boys make shoes and girls sew. She thought that business management was shared. The representative of the local footwear manufacturing association confirmed the gendered division of labor. Wives, he stated, handled the finances while husbands oversaw production. Women developed marketing strategies and men delivered shoes. In his firm, his wife showed samples to customers, received orders, and transacted product deliveries.

Mr. Smith, a community organizer, reported that in the local shoemaking businesses husbands supervised men and wives supervised women. He thought that the majority of wives marketed samples to department stores and bought raw materials while husbands prepared the patterns for design samples, managed the operation, finished products, and packed them for delivery. Mr. Anton, the owner of a large shoe business and a subcontractor, pointed out that his wife worked in the office and was responsible for supervising women. He supervised the men. His wife made purchase orders and marketed the products while he placed raw material orders and prepared the footwear patterns.

Not surprisingly, there was a division of responsibilities in household and child care duties. Household management remained a woman's domain. Women cooked the food, washed the clothes, and bore the major share of child care. Mr. and Mrs. Francis got up at 3 A.M. and husband waited with his daughter for her ride to work. Mrs. Francis prepared lunch for their sons. The representative of the local footwear manufacturing association said that women were in charge of household management. When I asked whether men performed more household tasks than 20 years ago, the representative said,

"Not much" because, men focus on the business. Mr. Anton sometimes picked his children up from school but his wife did the cooking. Mr. Smith confirmed that women were considered responsible for childcare, household activities, and both the family and business budgets.

WOMEN TRADE UNION ORGANIZERS IN BOTH INDONESIA AND THE PHILIPPINES

Trade union leaders are in the primary position to educate people on safe working conditions. Female workers need female trade union leaders for outreach. Yet, women trade union organizers and board members remain an anomaly. Trade unions by and large do not promote women's leadership. Some trade unions perceive women as weak and ineffective organizers and leaders. When women do get into organizing positions, marriage and work and family issues become a stumbling block. Even in the textile sector, where women workers outnumber men, there was one women union officer to every 10 men. An Indonesian trade union officer I interviewed said women were active until they got married.

> . . . after we give them training, try to educate them and increase their awareness, so that they could serve as organizers in the union. After a short while, they get married and disappear. (Male trade union representative, interviewed in Jakarta)

There are married women trade union leaders but it is a small percentage. An NGO representative remarked that not all husbands allowed their wives to work or continue being activists:

> . . . they (husbands) tend to think that women who are active in the (trade union) organization are rebellious—women who tend to rebel against men, especially if the man or the husband is not an activist or previously active in the organization. (Female NGO representative, interviewed in Jakarta)

Many successful female organizers are unmarried or separated. When asked how one of them coped with her work schedule and family life in the Philippines, she answered:

> I knew that it's coming. Okay. I was married when I started this job. Now I am a single mother of a son for the last 14 years. Here in the Philippines, it is also some sort of a trend, that successful women leaders are either single, separated, or with marital problems. I think this

is not only in the Philippines. (Female trade union representative, interviewed in Manila)

A male Philippine union organizer did not believe that there was an increased number of women in leadership positions and attributed this to women's multiple burdens of union work, work in the company, and domestic responsibilities:

> . . . they are not at all prepared to take on some of the positions because at the back of their mind, there are these responsibilities at work, and for my family. They would rather have responsibilities not at the top level but at the middle level where they think they would be more effective. But there are some women who have proven themselves as effective leaders and they have managed to overcome these challenges . . . maybe not at the industrial federation level, but at the local union level women are taking on these leadership positions. (Male trade union representative, interviewed in Manila)

Another Philippine female organizer thought that things had improved slightly. But, she described experiences all too familiar to women organizers:

> Gender campaign or gender education was not as highly acceptable (in the past) as it is now. I got frustrated with the trade union partners and bosses I had. This was because every time I got good results from my (projects), they will take away these projects from me and give them to the gentlemen. And then when these projects fail, they will return their management to me to rehabilitate them. The third time I was ordered to rehabilitate, I got out. (Another female trade union representative, interviewed in Manila)

CONCLUSION

This chapter has explored gendered dimensions within economic globalization, OSH, and home-based shoemaking. Home-based employment as part of global capitalism is having negative consequences—not only economic but any fundamental life aspects that depend on income earning: health, education, and power (Hennon & Locker, 2000).

Gender distinctions exist in the home-based shoe production in both countries. Men managed firms, were the major shareholders, and were the primary decision-makers. Men assembled shoes. Women stitched the uppers, dusted, made patterns on and cut material, applied glue, polished and cleaned the finished products, and folded boxes. Women earned less than men. My observations corroborated the view of Ms. Lazo that particularly small home-based family businesses revealed no sharp gender distinctions in the work tasks of men and women or the roles of husbands and wives. However, when the businesses grow larger, men become obvious managers and wives begin to engage in meticulous work tasks and stay frequently in the home while husbands go out of the house to do marketing or sales. One explanation is that a small business cannot afford to waste resources, therefore, both genders are needed in the management and manual labor tasks.

To be clear at the end: hazards in women's work have remained under-studied and under-estimated, therefore, the health consequences have remained under-reported and under-compensated (Messing, Dumais, & Romito, 1993). Women's work needs female organizers and female women trade union leaders who understand women's concerns.

REFERENCES

Bangser, M. (2002). Policy environments: Macroeconomics programming and par-ticipation. In G. Sen, A. George, & P. Östlin (Eds.), *Engendering international health: the challenge of equity* (pp. 257-280). Cambridge, MA: The MIT Press.

Brogan, K. (1994). *Women and children's health. Inside Indonesia: June.* Retrieved at: http://www.hamline.edu/apakabar/basisdata/1994/09/03/0000.html

Elson, D. (1983). Nimble fingers and other fables. In W. Chapkis & C. Enloe (Eds.), *Of common cloth: Women in the global textile industry* (pp. 5-14). Amsterdam: Transnational Institute.

Hartigan, P., Price J., & Tolhurst R. (2002). Communicable diseases: Outstanding commitments to gender and poverty. In G. Sen, A. George, & P. Östlin (Eds.), *Engendering international health: The challenge of equity* (pp. 37-62). Cambridge, MA: The MIT Press.

Hennon, C. B., & Loker, S. (2000). Gender and home-based employment in global economy. In C. B. Hennon, S. Loker, & R. Walker (Eds.), *Gender and home-based employment.* Westport, CT: Auburn House.

Karasek, R., & Theorell, T. (1990). *Healthy work: Stress, productivity, and recon-struction of working life.* New York: Basic Books Groupings.

Kemp, M. (2002). *Risky business—Women and occupational health.* Third World Network Features (first published in *Arrows for Change 7*(2), 2001). Retrieved at: http://dailynews.lk/2002/07/19/fea02.html

Messing, K. (1998). *One-eyed science: Occupational health and women workers.* Philadelphia, PA: Temple University Press.

Messing, K., Doniol-Shaw, G., & Haëntjens, C. (1994). Sugar and spice and every-thing nice: Health effects of the sexual division of labor among the train cleaners. In E. Fee & N. Krieger (Eds.), *Women's health, politics, and power: Essays on sex/gender, medicine, and public health* (pp. 155-169). Amityville, NY: Baywood.

Messing, K., Dumais, L., & Romito, P. (1993). Prostitutes and chimney sweeps both have problems: Towards full integration of both sexes in the study of occupational health. *Social Science and Medicine, 1,* 47-55.

Messing, K., Punnett, L., Bond, M., Alexanderson, K., Pyle, J., Zahm, S., et al. (2003). Be the fairest of them all: Challenges and recommendations for the treatment of gender in occupational health research. *American Journal of Industrial Medicine, 43*(6), 618-292.

Moran, T. H. (2002). *Beyond sweatshops: Foreign direct investment and globalization in developing countries.* Washington, DC: The Brookings Institutions Press.

Östlin, P. (2002). Examining work and its effects on health. In G. Sen, A. George, & P. Östlin (Eds.), *Engendering international health: The challenge of equity* (pp. 63-82). Cambridge, MA: The MIT Press.

Pyle, J. (1999). Third world women and global restructuring. In J. Chafetz (Ed.), *Handbook of the sociology of gender* (pp. 81-104). New York: Kluwer Academic/ Plenum Publishers.

Pyle, J. (2002). *Globalization, public policy, and the gendered division of labor.* Keynote Address at the Third International Congress on Women, Work & Health, Stockholm.

Quinn, M., Woskie, S., & Rosenberg, B. (2000). Women and work. In B. S. Levy & D. H. Wegman (Eds.), *Occupational health: Recognizing and preventing work-related disease and injury* (pp. 655-677). Philadelphia, PA: Lippincott Williams & Wilkins.

Sen, G., & Grown, C. (1987). *Development, crises, and alternative visions: Third world women's perspectives* (p. 34). New York: Monthly Review Press.

Standing, H. (2002). Frameworks for understanding health sector reform. In G. Sen, A. George, & P. Östlin (Eds.), *Engendering international health: The challenge of equity* (pp. 347-371). Cambridge, MA: The MIT Press.

Stellman, J. M. (1982). *Women's work, women's health: Myths and realities* (pp. 207-208). New York: Pantheon Books.

United Nations Development Programme (UNDP). (2003). Human development report. *Millennium development goals: A compact among nations to end human poverty.* New York: Oxford University Press (for the UNDP). Retrieved at: http://hdr.undp.org/en/reports/global/hdr2003/

United Nations Development Programme (UNDP). (2001). Indonesia: Human development report 2001. *Towards a new consensus: Democracy and human development in Indonesia.* Jakarta: UNDP.

Weix, G. C. (2000). Hidden managers at home: Elite Javanese women running New Order family firms. In J. Koning, M. Nolten, J. Rodenburg, & R. Saptari (Eds.), *Women and households in Indonesia: Cultural notions and social practices.* Surrey, UK: Nordic Institute of Asian Studies. Curzon Press.

Wolf, D. (2000). Beyond women and the household in Java: Reexamining the boundaries. In J. Koning, M. Nolten, J. Rodenburg, & R. Saptari (Eds.), *Women and households in Indonesia: Cultural notions and social practices.* Surrey, UK: Nordic Institute of Asian Studies. Curzon Press.

Wolf, D. L. (1992). *Factory daughters: Gender, household, and rural industrialization in Java.* Berkeley, CA: University of California Press.

Wooding, J., & Levenstein, C. (1999). *The point of production: Work environment in advanced industrial societies.* New York: The Guilford Press.

CHAPTER 5

Shoe Chemicals and Right-to-Know

CALL FOR SAFER CHEMICAL ALTERNATIVES

Why does shoe manufacturing still utilize hazardous solvent-based adhesives? Even though there have been promising results in introducing water-based shoe adhesives, the substitution effort has not taken off on a larger scale. Some manufacturers such as Nike have claimed that they have introduced water-based adhesives into their processes. In 1994, Kinney Shoe Corporation started full production at its Carlisle plant with the water-based adhesive, which required 6% of organic solvents to emulsify rubber particles (U.S. Environmental Protection Agency [US-EPA], 1998). The water-based adhesive has been called just as effective in bonding the shoe parts as the solvent-based adhesive, or even has improved product quality (US-EPA, 1998). A Korean company, NANOPOL, claimed its water-based NPA-8000 is a superior adhesive that is based on nanotechnology (NANOPOL, 2007). The adhesive is said to contain only water and solid polyurethane without any organic solvent, providing better performance because of its extremely fine particles and permeability. Furthermore, its use results in cost savings because less adhesive is used per shoe pair with NPA-8000 than with a solvent-based shoe (NANOPOL, 2007). When I discussed water-borne adhesives with enterprise managers, chemical engineers, and footwear factory personnel, their opinions varied. Supporters noted "yes, using water-based adhesives is possible, some modifications may need to be made in the process, but it is possible." The less supportive argued "water-based glues don't suit for shoes." A local small business owner I talked to in Marikina, the Philippines, asked:

81

Do you know who are not going to be very happy about the idea [of replacing solvents in footwear glues]?

Thus far, the petrochemical industry has supplied organic solvents for footwear adhesive and primer manufacturers.

WHERE ARE CHEMICAL LABELS AND DATA SHEETS?

More striking than the absence of water-based adhesives was the absence of proper labels and material safety datasheets (MSDSs) although they are regarded as fundamental principles of chemical safety practice. In curiosity to find out ingredients in existing solvent-based footwear adhesives, I placed different containers one next to another. All adhesive, primer, and other chemical containers—anywhere I went—lacked information about active ingredients. Even manufacturer contact information was often missing; in fact there were containers that did not mention the manufacturer at all and had only a brand name or an image on the cover. Some attempts were made to indicate health effects and precautions on the containers but these were rare cases in the midst of countless unacceptable examples. Both in Indonesia and the Philippines, labels were sometimes written only in the Chinese language. During a visit to a glue factory, I asked hosts why their containers were not labeled properly. They answered:

If we would put all skulls, crossbones, and dangers on our containers, no one would buy our products.

While in Thailand, I learned about the "adhesive container refill system." I was puzzled when told repeatedly: "The container doesn't hold what it says." Adhesive containers, once emptied, were returned to the same or a different chemical facility to be refilled. The refill did not necessarily contain the same product: it depended on the customer's orders. A tiny sticker label got attached to the container indicating the refilled adhesive type. Besides labels, the MSDS concept was unknown at shoe workshops and shoe supply stores. Even glue producers needed hours to retrieve an MSDS revealing that toluene is the primary footwear glue solvent.

RIGHT-TO-KNOW

In the 1980s, *right-to-know* laws emerged in the United States, most of which concern chemical exposure; Occupational Safety and Health Administration's (OSHA) Hazard Communication Standard is one of the regulations known as a *worker right-to-know* law (Ashford & Caldart, 1996), promulgated in 1983 and revised in 1994 (OSHA, 2007). Currently, it requires chemical suppliers to evaluate chemical hazards and provide information through labels and MSDSs. Employers in earlier times retained the right to determine when and if information on workplace chemicals should be made available to workers; information was considered "proprietary" and thus was unavailable for public scrutiny (Ashford & Caldart, 1996). Although *right-to-know* remains unpopular among American industry circles, it is accepted by them now as a fact of life, whereas the passage of such laws actually represented a kind of workplace democratization—mandatory sharing of information between management and labor (Ashford & Caldard, 1996). The rationale of right-to-know has been anchored on the following pillars: (a) moral rationale—similar to the concept of informed conset in medicine: the principle of personal autonomy, (b) economic rationale—grounded in the market efficiency concept to improve the quality of information on which decisions are based, and (c) political rationale, namely on worker empowerment (Ashford & Caldart, 1996). However, has the *right-to-know's* political rationale provided an atmosphere to confront existing employer-employee power inequalities in the workplace—besides *right-to-know,* have workers and citizens gained the necessary right-to-act (Rest, 2000)?

The *right-to-know* movement is a fledgling effort both in Indonesia and in the Philippines. Though none of my in-depth informants produced chemicals, they understood that chemical containers needed proper labels that spelled out ingredients, health hazards, and emergency measures. *Right-to-know* was viewed as embedded in OSH standards, management systems, union activities, and safety officers' functions. It was said that *right-to-know* should extend beyond controlling chemical exposures.

Indonesia adopted regulations for hazardous materials labeling in 1999 which required material safety data sheets. However, the regulations are not enforced. In many cases, workers do not understand what is written on the container labels and do not know how to protect themselves. An Indonesian employers' representative noted that all regulations related to chemical labels, datasheets, and pre-employment training had to be complied with: "workers need to be informed, trained, and explained clearly how to do first-aid." He believed that inspection walk-throughs should be taken seriously and that workers should be informed of the results.

> It is a must. Labeling and MSDSs, completely covered with information. We need, not only what chemical is, but what the substance really is, what is the effect for human being in acute and in chronic conditions and what is the antidote. And what is the emergency precaution that

should be picked by company and workers. What is first-aid procedure and others. But as I mentioned to you, if the chemical is produced in developing countries, sometimes the MSDS information is not completely there. (Employers' representative, interviewed in Jakarta)

Many people I talked with doubted that the government would prioritize worker right-to-know. An academic commented that engineering students had little knowledge of chemical safety regulations because the topics were rarely taught. If chemical engineering students lacked information, he wondered how could the general public be expected to know anything? Education is indeed essential here. An NGO representative affirmed that Indonesia needed an association for workplace accident victims because *right-to-know* is more comprehensive than just information on chemicals. When injured, many workers don't know how to complain or to file a claim for illnesses or injuries because noone advocates for the victims.

Mr. Saleh said that shoemakers had no choice of glues and even if they did, the alternatives were limited. He sometimes made glues from a latex-gasoline mixture, which was cheaper to use, but dangerous. When shoemakers could choose between safer, expensive glues and cheap glues, most of them selected the cheapest ones, the ones that were also more hazardous. Mr. Hakim recalled that in the 1960s safer *nabati* (vegetable) glues were available but they are not produced anymore. People I interviewed suggested that those who were invited to the ILO-IPEC training courses knew about chemical hazards. Part of the problem stems from the fact that bengkel owners do not pass down chemical safety and OSH information to *tukangs*. Though the coordinator of the Cibaduyut OSH Committee was not pleased about the presence of hazardous glues in home-based workshops, he knew that this practice would not be eliminated immediately. He hoped that the government would take action:

. . . how to reduce . . . to try to find [to] reduce the hazards . . . the community has the right to know about all of this. They actually know that those chemicals have bad smell, probably they also know that [they] have certain effects that affect their health condition. But they are compelled to work in this situation. Hazards affect the whole family. (Coordinator of the Cibaduyut OSH Committee, interviewed in Bandung)

In the Philippines, the Environmental Management Bureau (EMB) of the Department of Environment and Natural Resources (DENR) provides training for the pollution control officers and workers. The senior DENR officer mentioned that trainees became more aware about hazards and were eager to learn more:

And I could tell that based on the questions I get during my lectures now, as compared to the questions I got ten years back. I have been telling them about the Materials Safety Data Sheets for the last few years that I have been lecturing. By now, I hope they already have an idea that there should be an MSDS. Even in the households, I think people should be looking at the labels—what the labels say about what to do. I think everything should start at the home. (Senior DENR officer, interviewed in Manila)

Some manufacturers said that they supplied MSDSs, but others did not provide them. Even when provided, MSDSs are usually incomplete or inaccurate. Outreach to industries is considered a major challenge. The DENR officer suggested:

It is so hard to reach the other industries. We have an inter-agency committee. I don't know if we could have a combined inspection team with the Department of Labor, Department of Health, and the EMB. The EMB would look at the effects of chemicals to the environment. The Department of Labor would look at OSH. It is better to have this joint inspection. Even the small (manufacturers) here are saying that if the big manufacturing companies could not give MSDS, then why enforce these on smaller ones. They are saying that it is more difficult for them to come up with an MSDS. This is true. Some big companies would say to them: the labels are in Japanese, translate them. It has to be done by the bigger companies first because they have the resources and the capabilities to do these. Then, it would be easier for us to enforce this on the small manufacturers. (Senior DENR officer, interviewed in Manila)

A trade union organizer noted that worker *right-to-know* is part of Philippine OSH standards. In large, medium, and small companies the safety committee chair is always the CEO. Other committee members include the workers' or union representatives and a safety staff member. The point was to make sure that the safety and health committee is working, and not just on paper. For another trade union organizer, the crux of the problem was to demystify the labels and prepare them in laymen's language. One manual under development contained numerous incomprehensible terms. In her words:

. . . illnesses, these chemicals cause these illnesses . . . we don't even know what these illnesses are . . . and we have to explain to our members how using this word that this is basically what it means. So it's really a problem how chemistry terms can be translated into more understandable words, to be understood by people who have not studied chemistry. So that's one of our concerns also. When it comes to the garment industry, we have a lot of chemicals, we have a long list of chemicals used in the garment industry. But how can we inform our members that these chemicals cause these kinds of hazards; it is a problem and I don't know how we can solve that . . . and we have to hire very expensive people to explain what these chemicals are. So it's also a burden for trade unions to have this kind of training. Even if there is a bottle of chemical and has label on it that it contains this and that, so what? Even if I read it, it means nothing because I don't know what are these chemicals mentioned. (Trade union organizer, interviewed in Manila)

CONCLUSION

Attempts to link the right-to-know rationales (Ashford & Caldart, 1996)—moral, economic, and political—to the concept of the primary workplace hazard prevention have been weak at best if not non-existent. The *right-to-know* focus, especially hazards communication, needs more emphasis and shift toward safer materials substitution. It has importance for footwear production chiefly in urging substitution of water-based adhesives for solvent-based ones.

Shoe manufacturing is not only a hazardous undertaking itself but the life-cycle of a shoe goes back to extremely polluting and treacherous industries (tanning, chemicals production, and slaughterhouses). The global shoe industry has not internalized the primary prevention design concept from cradle to grave. For example, to what extent would it concern chemical suppliers and manufacturers that hazardous chemicals ultimately end up as footwear glues in homes and are used by family members, even children?

REFERENCES

Ashford, N. A., & Caldart, C. C. (1996). Technology, law, and the working environment (Rev. ed., pp. 309-310). Washington, DC: Island Press.

NANOPOL Inc. WWW-site. Product feature: Environmentally friendly NPA-8000 Series. Retrieved at: http://nanopol.com/eng/?view=products&sub=11

Occupational Safety and Health Administration (OSHA). Hazard communication. Retrieved at: http://www.osha.gov/SLTC/hazardcommunications/index.html

Rest, K. M. (2000). Ethics in occupational and environmental health. In B. Levy & D. Wegman (Eds.), Occupational health: Recognizing and preventing work-related disease and injury (p. 282). Philadelphia, PA: Lippincott, Williams, and Wilkins.

U.S. Environmental Protection Agency. (1998). Principles of pollution prevention and cleaner production: An International Training Course (China ed.). pp. 10-5–10-6. Retrieved at: http://www.p2pays.org/ref/02/01993.pdf

CHAPTER 6

The Way Forward

EXPANDING *THE POINT OF PRODUCTION* FRAMEWORK

This study of shoe-making has illustrated that use and handling of dangerous chemicals is intensified by globalization and associated with economic, political, social, and structural changes. When unsafe chemicals/materials are dispersed through society into areas with few resources and little safety and health infrastructure, highly hazardous conditions are produced.

The Point of Production described the hierarchical structure of U.S. formal sector workplaces (Wooding & Levenstein, 1999). Owners stand at the highest level, followed by managers, supervisors, and shopfloor workers (see Figure 1). Absent union power to boost workers' voice, owners and managers dominate decision-making on investments, production processes, and working conditions. Employers control the workplace, the worker, the technology and the hazard, while all others—insurance carriers, government agencies, unions, universities and other research institutes—gain industrial access through their relations to this central figure, the employer (Levenstein, Wooding, & Rosenberg, 2000).

In considering a developing country situation, the hierarchical power distribution is even more pronounced, especially in the informal sector. The poorest workers face the greatest risks when ever they attempt to organize or speak against to the power and authority of employers, contractors, and public authority. Industrial hygienists, engineers, and medical doctors cannot mitigate work place hazards in such an unbalanced social/political structure.

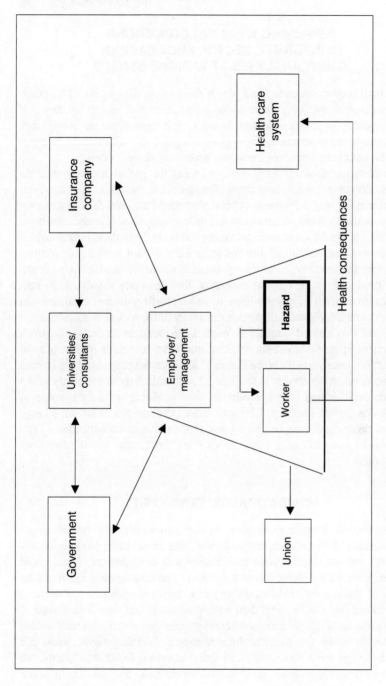

Figure 1. Actors in Occupational Safety and Health (3).
Source: Levenstein et al. (2000).

IMPROVING WORKING CONDITIONS
IN INFORMAL SECTOR SHOEMAKING:
AGENT ANALYSES AT VARIOUS STAGES

This final section expands *The Point of Production* critique into the globalized manufacturing setting where social pronouncements about the choice of technology (e.g., chemicals), as well as production method and the use of labor (e.g., home-based production), have grown flagrant as multinational corporations with their subcontracting networks have entered the model.

In review, the shoe industry consists of (a) the global industry with its retailers, designers, marketing firms, foreign shoe factories, and footwear associations; (b) major footwear buyers, manufacturers, and factories in producing countries; (c) raw material and technology suppliers; (d) subcontractors, managers, wholesalers, and intermediaries; and (e) at the bottom, homeworkers and their families. Responsibility for improving overall working conditions resides with the industry. Even though most footwear for industrialized countries is produced in developing countries, this does not absolve U.S. corporations from their responsibilities to ensure safe working conditions in supplier countries. Figure 2 illustrates the actors of the global shoe industry.

Here are two central questions: What is required to improve the work environment in home-based shoemaking and what role does gender play in this effort? An analysis chart (see Figure 3) has been developed to help answer these questions. All interveners of Figure 3, either directly or indirectly affect the work environment of a home-based shoe producer within the scope of the globalized shoe industry. Linkages offer possible places of *the change* where working conditions can be improved or interventions engendered. The below discussion elaborates the analysis from the bottom up, starting from homeworkers.

HOMEWORKERS' COMMUNITY

There are numerous organizations at the community level which might help home-based shoemakers to raise awareness about safer working conditions, and perhaps also improve their home-work environment. These could distribute information about solvents and glues and raise knowledge about the dangers of home work. Homeworkers can improve working conditions to a limited extent, but this requires their having access to adequate information.

With awareness raised, homeworkers' interventions depend on their access to money to make the required improvements. Warning signs, work and material storage areas separated from living quarters, safety workshops, the switch over to less toxic glues, and regular housekeeping cost something. Some

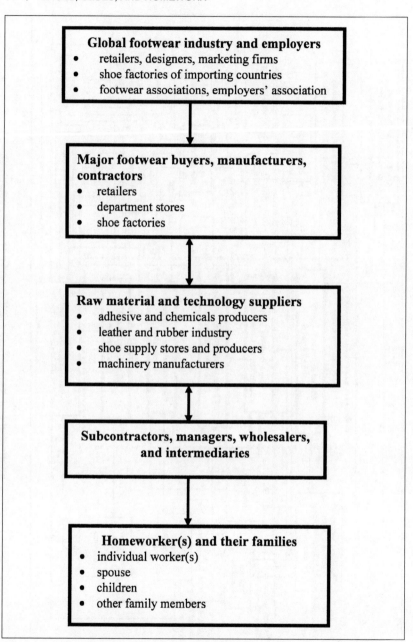

Figure 2. Global footwear industry actors.

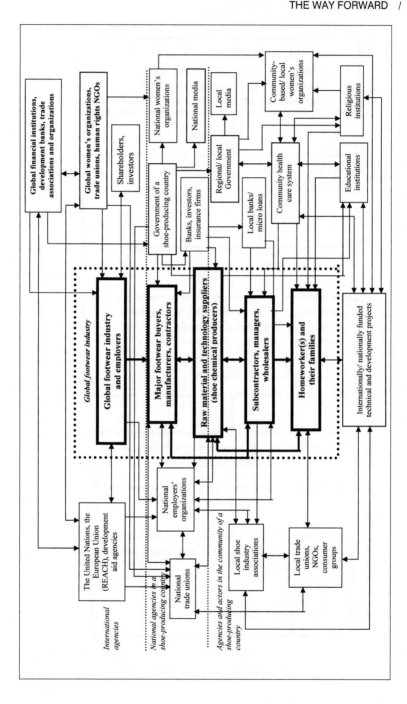

Figure 3. Informal sector shoe industry actors and potential interveners.

Biñan homeworkers labeled chemical containers themselves. But, the provision of full information, including labeling and MSDSs, remains the primary responsibility of chemical manufacturers and suppliers—they after all do know what they have produced.

Maternity and early childhood care units in Bandung and Biñan are potential vehicles for community-based *right-to-know* advocacy. In Indonesia, the government's immunization programs are likely focal points as well. Because workers and their families visit community health care facilities, these spaces offer a place where women in particular might feel most comfortable to voice their concerns and seek advice about workplace health and safety.

Educational institutions and locally situated development projects play an important role as communicators and builders of a hazard communication infrastructure. For example, Mr. Hiet noted that shoemaking communities needed instruction at the junior high school level focused on safe shoemaking and other issues pertaining to industry. This could be an efficient way to tackle the child labor. Universities work with NGOs to study health and safety issues.

A trade union organizer from the Philippines pointed out that once workers received safety and health training, they usually did not have a chance to apply their new knowledge in the practice. Training needs to be linked to workplace change. Interviewees mentioned that education is essential so that collective bargaining becomes more focused on working conditions. Professional level positions for industrial hygienists, safety officers, and occupational medicine practitioners, and policy-makers are critical at workers' organizations.

Often, an outside intervener is required to instigate the change. In both countries, the chief change agent in initiating work environment improvements in informal sector shoe-making has been the ILO-IPEC Footwear Program (i.e., national/international development projects, Figure 3). In Bandung, the ILO-IPEC Footwear Program helped to establish an OSH Committee, organized training, and applied the ILO-PATRIS[1] methodology in their day-to-day workplace monitoring work. With the Bandung Institute of Technology, the ILO-IPEC renovated two *bengkels* and improved working conditions by supplying fans, better lighting, and sturdier chairs with backrests. In Biñan, the ILO-IPEC Footwear Program in cooperation with the OSH Center of the Philippines organized OSH training courses, developed training and advocacy materials, and produced a video.

---

[1]PATRIS stands for Participatory Action Training for Informal Sector Operators.

THE NATIONAL LEVEL

The government is the gatekeeper for most NGO international activity. It has enforcement power and can influence national agencies, the industry representatives, workers' and women's organizations, lenders and insurance companies, regional and local governments, and community-based organizations. The ILO 2002 Conference Report states: *Government policies and legislation are key elements in supporting or eroding collective representation and social dialogue in the informal economy of those in the informal economy* (ILO, 2002). The government can compel work space improvements through policy, enforcement, research, and advocacy. But, such interventions are not taking place because of politics, limited budgets and facilities, and too small staffs to affect the thousands of small shops scattered across both countries.

The mass media can communicate health and safety information. In 2003, newspapers, television stations, and radio programs covered stories on the impact of globalization and free trade on workers. Sweatshop working conditions, export processing zones, and the effects of trade laws on workers were analyzed.

Employers' organizations and trade unions at the national level have important roles to play advocating for worker protections. But too often their agendas excluded safety and health issues. Wages, benefits, and keeping a job often overshadowed safe work discussions. When accidents happened, workers blamed themselves. Innovative, fresh, and creative strategies to reach out to homeworkers through TV programs, awareness-raising campaigns, and activities like street theaters are essential (ILO, 2002). Employers' strategies for reaching informal workers consist of the establishment of entrepreneurship development institutes, and corporate social responsibility initiatives (ILO, 2002).

INTERNATIONAL AGENTS AND INITIATIVES

Much intervention must take place at the international level outside of the shoemaking community. Even the most well crafted work environment laws and policies will have limited meaning unless they are supported financially and backed up in the political process.

To improve working conditions in shoe manufacturing (or any other manufacturing sectors), it is pertinent that major financial institutions become involved in work environment initiatives to uproot the misperceptions that OSH policies, programs, and preventive interventions against job hazards are costly practices for enterprises and societies. The international financial institutions are in a decisive position to fortify government social and health infrastructures and the production methods of the global and local shoe industry.

In the absence of sufficient government infrastructure and trade union advocacy for safety in the informal sector—like home-based shoemaking—the role of women and the value of organizing women are crucial to promote safer production systems.

The United Nations (UN) agencies such as the ILO, the WHO, the United Nations Women's Fund (UNIFEM), the UNEP, the United Nations Industrial Development Organization (UNIDO), and others continue their essential functions in setting up international standards, policy and advocacy tools, and carrying out technical and development cooperation programs. The problem lies in the lack of enforcement power over their standards and framework agreements. In addition, their financial resources are often limited unless linked to external funds. Despite the absence of the standard enforcement power, the UN agencies' overall audience to influence through awareness-raising and capacity-building is enormous. Although understanding the sovereignty concerns, an appropriate international agency is needed to monitor states on issues related to fundamental human rights—and when necessary, pressure the states to enforce and apply international standards.

The UN's International Programme on Chemical Safety, the International Coordinating Committee on the Sound Management of Chemicals, the Intergovernmental Forum on Chemical Safety, and the like have all carried out laudable efforts in developing chemical safety policies, safety cards, information sheets, databases, manuals, etc to address safer use of chemicals. In 2002, the UN adopted its *Globally Harmonized System of Classification and Labeling of Chemicals* addressing (a) chemicals classification according to hazard types and (b) harmonized chemicals hazard communication methods, including labels and material safety data sheets. The purpose is to provide hazard and toxicity information for improved protection of human and environmental health when handling, transporting and using chemicals. It also offers a framework for harmonizing chemicals rules and regulations, for example to facilitate international trade (UNECE, 2002).

In December 2006, the European Union (EU) adopted the regulation on Registration, Evaluation, Authorization, and Restriction of Chemicals (REACH). The industry—manufacturers and importers—have now greater responsibility for managing the chemical risks, provide safety information, and register the information in the central database located in the newly established European Chemicals Agency (ECHA) in Helsinki. REACH also requires a substitution plan for chemicals when suitable safer alternatives exist (EC, 2007). REACH is one of the most innovative and comprehensive international chemicals program to date and can have a major impact both in the EU and beyond.

Following the UK and Australian policies and practices for eliminating occupational hazards at the source, the U.S. National Institute of Occupational Safety and Health (NIOSH) launched the national Prevention through Design (PtD) initiative in 2007. It is gaining enthusiastic support, especially from various U.S. industry branches. The initiative urges us to implement effective primary prevention measures rather than controlling exposures. The NIOSH-PtD premise is defined as: Addressing occupational safety and health needs in the design process to prevent or minimize the work-related hazards and risks associated with the construction, manufacture, use, maintenance, and disposal of facilities, materials, and equipment (US-NIOSH, 2007). It remains to be seen how seriously and largely U.S. manufacturers embrace the PtD concept and apply it to their overseas production processes.

CONCLUSION

This study has looked at safety and health practices in informal sector shoemaking—within the framework of the globalized shoe manufacturing industry. An analysis was carried out to identify potential intervention points to improve the work environment. It has suggested agents to whom homeworkers themselves could turn to, voice concerns, and seek advice as well as potential international, national, and local interveners that could influence working conditions in the informal sector through policy implementation measures.

Major responsibility for health and safety must be borne by the most prominent and profitable shoe companies. But, this has not happened. Who else could fill this role? At the national level, the central government but so long as its social and health infrastructures are restricted by financial considerations the unsafe work in the informal sector will not be improved.

International human rights groups, NGOs, and women's organizations have achieved notable results although many question how sustainable their achievements are. Local unions and women's groups (like Self Employed Women's Association (SEWA)) offer encouraging examples. Nonetheless, it is unrealistic to assume that home-based manufacturers—whether shoe workers or any other producers—will build trade unions in the near term. Movement-building appears more realistic when various international trade union secretariats, women's organizations, and community-based organizations combine forces. At the community level, health care providers, educational institutions, and neighborhood-based technical and economic development projects can promote workplace change. But again, health care and educational institutions are dependent on the government resources.

If the government and unions remain weak, it is necessary to look out where the potential power, thus, the potential change agent, resides. Recently, company shareholders have not been pleased to find their investments being used for manufacturing toxic consumer products. As an example, the Mattel shareholders raised a law suit against the company over the toxic, lead-painted toys. Similarly, would investors elsewhere accept their companies' products or services being toxic or otherwise unsafe? However, they still accept everyday consumer products, like shoes, being produced in hazardous working conditions. Will hazardous working conditions ever receive the same attention as hazardous consumer products?

As long as organic solvents are being used, shoe manufacturing remains a hazardous work. "Why does shoe manufacturing utilize hazardous solvent-based adhesives instead of safer water-based ones?" has been the key question throughout the study. There aren't simple answers but one answer could be because most influential actors in Figure 3 allow the status quo to continue. What kind of OSH policy measures should we then recommend for the informal sector? It's rather clear now that regulating the informal economy is not a solution, instead, formalizing the informal is—or as De Soto put it "legalizing the extralegal" (De Soto, 2000).

REFERENCES

De Soto, H. (2000). *The mystery of capital: Why capitalism triumphs in the West and fails everywhere else* (p. 21). New York: Basic Books.

European Commission (EC), Directorate General of Environment. (2007). REACH. Retrieved at: http://ec.europa.eu/environment/chemicals/reach/reach_intro.htm

International Labour Office (ILO). (2002). Decent work and the informal economy. International Labour Conference, 90th Session. ILO, Geneva. Retrieved at: http://www.ilo.org/public/libdoc/ilo/2002/102B09_133_engl.pdf

Levenstein, C., Wooding, J., & Rosenberg, B. (2000). Occupational health: Social perspective. In B. S. Levy & D. H. Wegman (Eds.), *Occupational health: Recognizing and preventing work-related disease and injury* (pp. 27-50). Philadelphia, PA: Lippincott Williams & Wilkins.

United Nations Economic Commission for Europe. (2002). Globally harmonized system of classification and Labeling of chemicals (GHS). Retrieved at: http://www.unece.org/trans/danger/publi/ghs/ghs_welcome_e.html

U.S. National Institute of Occupational Safety and Health (NIOSH). Centers for Disease Control and Prevention (CDC). Prevention through Design website: http://www.cdc.gov/niosh/topics/ptd/

Wooding, J., & Levenstein, C. (1999). *The point of production: Work environment in advanced industrial societies.* New York: The Guilford Press.

Index

Accident certification, 48
Acetone, 23-25
Adhesives, solvent-based, 27-28, 96
 See also Chemicals used in
  home-based production; Hazards,
  shoemaking and its
Adidas, 5
Africa, 44, 45
Albania, 45
American Apparel & Footwear
 Association (AAFA), 4
Argentina, 45
Arroyo, Gloria, 6, 12
Asian Development Bank (ADB), 3
Australia, 95

Bandung, 6-9
Benzene, 24, 25, 27-28
Beyond Sweatshops (Moran), 64
Biñan (the Philippines), 10
Bladder cancer, 25
Blanc, Paul, 24
Bowerman, Bill, 24-25
Brazil, 4
Butanol, 25
Buying agents, 1-3

Cancer, 25-26
Catholic Church, 73
Central nervous system and exposure to
 solvents, 24-25

Chemicals used in home-based
 production
 alternatives, call for safer chemical,
  81-82
 Environmental Management
  Bureau, 84
 future trends/the way forward, 94,
  96
 gender issues, 65
 labels and data sheets, where are
  the, 82, 83
 overview, xiv-xv
 right-to-know issues, 82-86
 summary/conclusions, 86
 water-based adhesives, 81-82
 See also Hazards, shoemaking and
  its
Child care, household duties and,
 71-72, 75-76
Child workers, 7, 28-29, 37
China, 4-6, 27-28
Chloroprene, 26
Cigarette smoking, 33
Condom use, 73
Crafts production, 46
Cyclohexane, 24

Democracy/government, free
 marketeers minimizing role of, vi
DEPNAKER, 48, 49
De Soto, Hernando, 44
Dewi, S. E., 7
Dichloroethylene, 24

Dichloromethane, 23, 24
Digestive system cancer, 25
Diisocyanate, 24
DK3N, 48
DNA damage, 26
Dust, grinding, 32

Education, children and work *vs.,* 7
Education (worker) needed to improve
    working conditions, 92
Employment and global production, 3-4
Estrella-Gust, D. P., 28-29
Ethanol, 25
Ethyl acetate, 23, 25
European Union (EU), 94

Finland, 45
Fire, 23, 32
Forrant, Robert, v-vii
Future trends/the way forward
    actors of global shoe industry, 89, 90
    analysis chart for improving working
        conditions, 89, 91
    chemicals used in home-based
        production, 94, 96
    community, homeworkers', 89, 92
    expanding the *Point of Production*
        framework, 87-88
    hierarchical power distribution, 87-88
    international agents and initiatives,
        93-94
    national level, 93
    summary/conclusions, 95-96

Gender issues
    Catholic Church, 73
    chemical exposures, 65
    child care, household duties and, 71-72,
        75-76
    chronic injuries, 65
    division of labor and home-based
        business management, 67-69, 73-76

[Gender issues]
    employment and global production,
        3-4
    finances and managing the business,
        69-70
    government leadership/technical
        specialist positions, 72-73
    harassment, sexual/general,
        72
    health/well-being of women and
        economic globalization, 64
    Indonesia, reflections from,
        66-72
    informal sector/economy,
        45-47
    occupational safety and health,
        64-67
    overview, 63
    the Philippines, reflections from the,
        72-76
    Self-Employed Women's
        Association, 57-58, 95
    skilled shoemakers, why aren't
        women, 70-71
    summary/conclusions, 77-78
    sustainability and economic
        development, vi-vii
    union organizers, female, 76-77
    wages, 4, 65-66
    women as desired industrial
        workers, 45-47
    Women in Informal Employment
        Globalizing and Organizing,
        57-58
Germany, 26
Globalization, impacts of, 1-4, 44, 64,
        89-90
    See also Structure of global
        footwear industry; *individual*
        subject headings
    Globally Harmonized System of
        Classification and Labeling of
        Chemicals, 94
Grinding and dust, 32
Guatemala, 56

Hazards, shoemaking and its
  benzene, 27-28
  cancer studies, 25-26
  child shoemakers, 28-29, 37
  co-exposures, solvent, 26-27
  fire, 23, 32
  future trends/the way forward, 95
  interview findings (Indonesia), 35-37
  interview findings (the Philippines),
    38-39
  liver damage, 27
  nervous system effects, 24-25
  observations, walk-through, 31-35
  posture, work, 33, 35
  process in home-based workshops,
    29-31
  reproductive health issues, 26
  respiratory health issues, 25, 32
  solvent and dust exposures worldwide,
    23
  storage of toxic/flammable chemicals,
    23, 32, 33, 37
  summary/conclusions, 39-40
  ventilation, 32, 33
  See also Chemicals used in
    home-based production; Gender
    issues
Health. *See* Chemicals used in
    home-based production; Gender
    issues; Safety and health
    infrastructure, Indonesian/the
    Philippines' work
Heptane, 24
Hexane, 23-25, 27, 34
Hierarchical power distribution, 87-88
HIPERKES, 48
HIV/AIDS, 73
Home-based production, viii-xi, xiii, xiv,
    29-31
  See also Informal sector/economy;
    individual subject headings
HomeNET, 58
Hong Kong, 6
Household duties and child care, 71-72,
    75-76

ILO-IPEC (International Labour
    Organization- International
    Programme on the Elimination of
    Child Labour) Rapid Assessment
    study, 6-7
India, 57-58
Indonesia, 3
  See also individual subject headings
Industrial home work/outwork, 46
Informal sector/economy
  attributes of, three distinctive,
    43-44
  Bureau of Working Conditions, 53,
    54
  defining terms, 45-46
  Department of Labor and
    Employment, 52-53
  environment, work, 50-51, 55-57
  Indonesia, reflections from, 47-52
  invisibility dilemma, 55
  organizing the workers, 57-58
  OSH Center established in 1992,
    52-54
  overview, 43
  Peruvian workers, 44
  the Philippines, reflections from the,
    52-57
  safety/health infrastructure, work,
    47-49, 52-57
  social protection, 55-56
  statistics on, 44-45
  subcontracting, 45
  summary/conclusions, 58
  women as desired industrial
    outworkers, 45-47
  Women in Informal Employment
    Globalizing and Organizing,
    44-45
Institute for Liberty and Democracy
    (ILC), 44
Institute of Labour Studies (ILS), 57
International Agency for Research on
    Cancer (IARC), 25
International Conference of Women in
    Beijing (1995), 57

International Labour Organization (ILO),
xiii, 6-7, 25, 43, 45, 52-53, 92, 93
International Programme on the
Elimination of Child Labour (IPEC),
xiii, 6-7, 28, 31, 37, 84, 92
Invisibility dilemma and informal work
environment, 55
Ireland, 45
Italy, 3

Kemp, Melody, 66
Kinney Shoe Corporation, 81
Korea, South, 3, 4

Labels, chemical, 82, 83
*Labour Practices in the Footwear,
Leather, Textiles and Clothing
Industries,* 3
Latin America, 44-45
Lazo, Lucita, 55
Legislation
(Indonesia) Health Law No. 23 of
1992, 48
(Indonesia) Manpower Act of 2003,
49
(Indonesia) Work Safety Act of 1970,
47-48, 66
(the Philippines) Constitution of 1987,
52
(the Philippines) Labor Code of 1974,
52
(the Philippines) National Health
Insurance Law of 1995, 56
Leukemia, 25
Levenstein, Charles, v-vii
Liver damage, 27

Marikina (the Philippines), 10
Market forces minimizing role of
democracy/government, vi
Markkanen, Pia, v, vi
Marquina, 10

Massachusetts Health Inspection
Report (1912), 39-40
Material safety datasheets (MSDSs),
82, 83, 85
Methyl-ethyl-ketone (MEK), 23-25,
27
Mexico, 3, 4, 45
Middle East, 44
Mother and Child Care Community
Based Integrated Project (MCC),
56
Multiple myeloma, 25-26

NANOPOL, 81
Nasal cancer, 25
National Institute for Occupational
Safety and Health (NIOSH), 95
Nervous system and exposure to
solvents, 24-25
Netherlands, 45
Newsweek International, 10
N-heptane, 24
N-hexane, 23, 24
Nike, 5, 81
Non-Hodgkin's lymphoma, 26
Nutrition issues, 51
Nuwa Wea, Jacob, 48

Occupational Safety and Health
Administration (OSHA), 82-83
Occupational Safety and Health
Center (OSH Center) of the
Philippines, 28, 52-54
Organization for Education Resources
and Training (ORT), 56

Parasitic diseases, 51
PATAMABA, 58
PATRIS (Participatory Action
Training for Informal Sector
Operators), 92

Peru, 44
Philippine Footwear Federation, 6
the Philippines. *See individual subject headings*
Photographs of production process, viii-xi, xiii
Point of Production, 87-89
Polluted environments, vi
Polyneuropathy, 24-25
Polyvinyl chloride (PVC), 24
Portugal, 3
Posture, work, 33, 35
Prevention through Design (PtD), 95
Production process, photographs of, viii-xi, xiii
Profit margins, 9
Protests, labor, 5
PT Doson, 5

Reebok, 5
Registration, Evaluation, Authorization, and Restriction of Chemicals (REACH), 94
Religion, 73
Reproductive health issues, 26, 64, 66, 73
Respiratory health issues, 25, 32
Right-to-know issues, chemicals and, 82-86
Ron, Aviva, 56

Safety and health infrastructure, Indonesian/the Philippines' work, 47-49, 52-57
See also Chemicals used in home-based production; Gender issues; Hazards, shoemaking and its
Self-Employed Women's Association (SEWA), 57-58, 95
Shoemaker's polyneuropathy, 24-25
Social protection and informal work environment, 55-56
Soekarnoputri, Megawati, 48

Solvents, organic. *See* Chemicals used in home-based production; Gender issues; Hazards, shoemaking and its
South Africa, 45
Storage of toxic/flammable chemicals, 23, 32, 33, 37
Structural adjustment programs (SAPs), 64
Structure of global footwear industry
Bandung (Indonesia), 6-9
bengkels and tukangs, 7-8
chain, global production, 1-3
children and work *vs.* education, 7
customers, 8-9
employment and global production, 3-4
imported shoes into the Philippines, dilemma of, 12-13
Indonesia, exports from, 4-5
interdependencies among people/communities/nations, 1
Marikina/Biñan (the Philippines), 10-14
nature of local industry in the Philippines, 11-12
the Philippines, exports from, 5-6
profiles of interviewed shoemakers/producers, 15-20
profit margins, 9
summary/conclusions, 14
U.S. based athletic shoe industry, 3
wages, 9, 13-14
Subcontracting, 45
Survival and informal sector attributes, 43-44
Sustainability and economic development, vi-vii

Taiwan, 4
Thailand, viii-xi, xiii, 4
Tokman, V., 43
Toluene, 23-27
Tomei, M., 45

Ulil Albab Health Foundation, 28-29
Union organizers, female, 76-77
United Kingdom, 95
United Nations, 67, 73, 94
United Shoe Machinery Company, 4
U.S. based athletic shoe industry, 3, 4

Ventilation, 32, 33
Viet Nam, 4, 5

Wages, 4, 9, 13-14, 65-66
Water-based adhesives, 81-82, 96
Wea, Jacob Nuwa, 48

White-collar homeworkers, 46
Wolf, Diane, 69
Women in Informal Employment
    Globalizing and Organizing
    (WIEGO), 44-45, 57-58
Wooding, John, v-vii
*Working Condition for Special Groups
    of Employees,* 52
Working poor and informal sector
    attributes, 43
World Bank, 49

Xylene, 24
Xylenol, 25

In Praise

This book highlights the importance of substituting hazardous chemicals with safer alternatives. Dr. Markkanen's research shows that globalized production systems and markets have created situations in which the use and disposal of toxic chemicals occurs in some countries and consumption of the final products in others. Global elimination or minimization of chemical hazards requires connecting local conditions to effective preventive programs at the international level of chemicals management.

Dr. Margaret Quinn
Professor, Department of Work Environment
University of Massachusetts Lowell

Around the world, women work from their homes to produce shoes, garments, electronic goods, soccer balls, and countless other products for the global economy. In the process, their homes become workplaces and their families are exposed to occupational safety and health risks. Shoemaking is a particularly hazardous occupation for women and their families. This pioneering book by Pia Markkanen documents the dangers to women and their families of working in the global footwear industry, notably the exposure to chemical solvents and dust. Use of chemicals and other occupational health and safety risks associated with home-based production is not limited to shoe-making. Whether or not they work alongside their mothers, the children of home-based women workers, in the footwear and other industries, share the health and safety risks faced by their mothers. A global economy that relies so heavily on home-based production by women workers needs to take stock of and be held accountable for the occupational safety and health risks associated with global production— all the way down the global production chain to the home-based producers, mainly women, at the bottom of the chain. This book is a must read for anyone concerned about decent work and economic justice in today's global economy.

Marty Chen
Lecturer in Public Policy, Harvard Kennedy School
Manufacturing International Coordinator, WIEGO Network

This book takes the reader from the home-based realities of shoe to the sophisticated global scenario.

Dr. Dulce P. Estrella-Gust
Executive Director, Occupational Safety and Health Center
Quezon City, Philippines

A SELECTION OF TITLES FROM THE

WORK, HEALTH AND ENVIRONMENT SERIES

Series Editors, *Charles Levenstein, Robert Forrant and John Wooding*

AT THE POINT OF PRODUCTION
The Social Analysis of Occupational
and Environmental Health
Edited by Charles Levenstein

BEYOND CHILD'S PLAY
Sustainable Product Design in the
Global Doll-Making Industry
Sally Edwards

ENVIRONMENTAL UNIONS
Labor and the Superfund
Craig Slatin

METAL FATIGUE
American Bosch and the Demise
of Metalworking in the Connecticut River Valley
Robert Forrant

SHOES, GLUES AND HOMEWORK
Dangerous Work in the Global Footwear Industry
Pia Markkanen

WITHIN REACH?
Managing Chemical Risks in Small Enterprises
David Walters

INSIDE AND OUT
Universities and Education for Sustainable Development
Edited by Robert Forrant and Linda Silka

WORKING DISASTERS
The Politics of Recognition and Response
Edited by Eric Tucker

LABOR-ENVIRONMENTAL COALITIONS
Lessons from a Louisiana Petrochemical Region
Thomas Estabrook

CORPORATE SOCIAL RESPONSIBILITY
FAILURES IN THE OIL INDUSTRY
Edited by Charles Woolfson and Matthias Beck

For Product Safety Concerns and Information please contact our
EU representative GPSR@taylorandfrancis.com Taylor & Francis
Verlag GmbH, Kaufingerstraße 24, 80331 München, Germany